Joyous Adventure

Joyous Adventure

Sermons for the Christian Year

BY DAVID ALEXANDER MacLENNAN

 Harper & Brothers Publishers New York

FOR

Ann, Effie, Neil and Colin

Contents

Introduction

Absolutely fearless, always getting into trouble, and absurdly happy is the description of the first Christians given by a competent scholar of our time. This high tribute by the late Dr. T. Reavely Glover is not extravagant. In the morning years of the Christian Church and in every subsequent period men and women of diverse temperament and background have found in Christ the secret of valiant and joyful living.

Today we hear much of secular despair. Not enough is heard of the Good News of God's action in Jesus Christ whereby He has visited and redeemed His people. Always Christian preaching must realistically confront men and women with the tragic facts of life. Christian preaching also must make possible our confrontation by the glorious God who has achieved our deliverance from spiritual and moral enemies in what T. S. Eliot calls "this twittering world." Despite intellectual assent to the sublime truths of the Faith, we live as "hollow men" because we refuse to engage in the joyous adventure to which our victorious Lord calls us. This is the exacting and exhilarating adventure of co-operating with His Spirit and purpose for the creation of Christlike personalities and community everywhere in the inhabited earth.

To indicate the goals, point out some of the guideposts and show how we may find and follow Him who is the unfailing resource of wisdom, courage and joy, are objectives of all Christian preaching.

These sermons are offered as expressions of one preacher's attempt to achieve these high objectives. A few of the sermons that follow were given in the closing months of my ministry at Timothy Eaton Memorial Church, Toronto, Ontario. For the loving expectancy and patience with which the members of that congregation heard the messages I give thanks to God and to them. Other sermons in this book were preached in various churches and college chapels during the past three years. In this period my ministry has been that of a modern circuit rider with headquarters at an interdenominational school of the prophets. All who made possible the privilege of preaching Christ to so many I hold "in my heart as partakers with me of grace . . . in the defense and confirmation of the Gospel."

Themes have been suggested by the central truths of the Gospel celebrated in the great days and seasons of the Christian Year. Advent, Christmas, Lent, Easter, Pentecost and other significant occasions are more than milestones on the year's road; such days commemorate events in time and eternity. They shine as beacons of unfailing light to direct the traveler on his road to the City of God.

Grateful appreciation is expressed to the authors, agents and publishers for gracious permission to quote from their publications.

The Christian Century Pulpit has graciously given consent to include two sermons which appeared in its pages, "I Saw Two Calvaries" and "Why the Church?"; *Christian Herald* has extended the same courtesy in connection with "Questions Before the House." "Only the Truth Remains" was originally prepared for radio presentation through the Canadian Broadcasting Corporation on the darkest Good Friday of World War II; "Present—Tense; Future—Perfect" was delivered in the Sunday Evening Hour program of the Canadian Broadcasting Corporation, Ottawa, Ontario, on Easter Day, 1951.

DAVID ALEXANDER MACLENNAN

The Divinity School, Yale University
New Haven, Connecticut
May, 1952

Joyous Adventure

1

Basic Christianity

God was in Christ reconciling the world to Himself, not counting their trespasses against them, and entrusting to us the message of reconciliation.
2 CORINTHIANS 5:19 (R.S.V.)

TAXICAB drivers frequently startle their passengers. This effect is achieved mainly but not exclusively by their daring maneuvers in traffic. In some instances their conversational gambits surprise the stranger. It was so during a ride from a church to a synagogue where an interfaith meeting was held. We were hurtling through cars, trucks and pedestrians as if the cab was a jet plane five miles up. Suddenly in that disconcerting fashion skillful pilots of such vehicles have, my driver turned his head and asked, "What is there in this religion business? Tell me what Christianity is in a few words. I don't want a sermon. I'd just like a quick answer." It was a tall order. How would you have answered him?

Definitions of Christianity are many and varied. Most of them are true as far as they go. Between world wars much was made of the axiom that Christianity is not assent to a form of words but consent to a way of life. Creedal statements were then unpopular, and theological pronouncements fell into disrepute in many quarters. Ethical emphasis was deemed paramount. So a thoughtful Christian woman wrote a quarter of a century ago that Christianity consists of the thought, spirit and conduct in the world traceable to Jesus' life and teachings. Earlier a noble and influential German scholar, Dr. Adolph Harnack, said that Christianity is essentially life lived in the midst of time under the light and by the help of eternity. More recently Dr. Will Durant expressed

13

preference for interpreting Christianity as the "sincere acceptance of the moral ideals of Christ."

It is wise to go back to the literary sources of our religion. The New Testament is the chief source and in its pages we may discover what the first Christians considered to be basic Christianity.

For the early Church, and for the Church today, the center of the Faith, the heart of the Christian way, was something more than acceptance of lofty ethical principles, although being a Christian involved ethical obedience. It was more than observance of ritual requirements, and even intellectual assent to a sublime philosophy of life. These elements were implied. New Testament Christianity centered in a Person, and that Person was Jesus Christ. Yet Christianity is more than the effort to imitate Jesus. What is the heart of it?

Here is one classic answer, set down by a keen, cultured mind. Once he had been a determined and deadly antagonist of the Faith he later embraced and advocated. Paul's statement of basic Christianity was this: "God was in Christ reconciling the world to Himself." Read the entire fifth chapter of his second letter to the Corinthian church if you would grasp the audacious claim he made. Now, however, let those four words blaze in your mind and imagination: *"God—was—in—Christ."*

First let us realize that *this is a tremendous claim.* If, like most of us, you have been exposed to Christian teaching it may not seem tremendous. Actually to hear that declaration for the first time, and to learn that it was made by an intelligent and informed person as a serious statement of fact, would be as revolutionary as the announcement a few years ago that the atom had been cracked open and its incalculable energy released for man's use. Does someone say, What is so revolutionary about Paul's announcement? If we believe in God and that He has personal dealings with His human creatures, if we know anything about the character and influence of Jesus of Nazareth, can we not agree that God was in Him? The divine was assuredly in this young prophet of Galilee who went about doing good, who healed the sick, taught the way of love, resisted entrenched evil and remained loyal to the truth as He saw it until His loyalty earned Him a martyr's death. God is in every human being. Does not the New Testament teach that God is the light that lighteth every man who comes into the world? "Yes," says a typical broad-minded twentieth century citizen, "I am prepared to acknowledge that the divine Spirit was unmistakably present in the personality of the Galilean teacher of long ago."

But the Christianity of the New Testament, of the main line of the Church's teaching across nineteen centuries, means more than that. As one has said, the Christian religion is something more than a matter of academic interest in a vivid personality of antiquity. Christianity is Christ, God in a human life, like us and yet unlike us. God has uniquely and savingly disclosed Himself in this man. His self-revelation was through a man completely human and yet indubitably divine. Other religions have their man-gods, but here is One who was truly man, and yet who was conscious of His unique relationship to the Love that moves the sun and all the stars. If you read Arnold Toynbee's *A Study of History* you will recall the section entitled "The God Incarnate in a Man." This philosopher-historian writes of the way in which Jesus broke "right away from the conventional line of action taken by other would-be saviours." He asks what distinguishes Him from all others, and answers:

> The answer is that these others knew themselves to be no more than men, whereas Jesus was a man who believed himself to be the Son of God. . . . "The One remains, the many change and pass." . . . As we stand and gaze with our eyes fixed upon the farther shore, a single figure rises from the flood and straightway fills the whole horizon. There is the Saviour; "and the pleasure of the Lord shall prosper in his hand; he shall see of the travail of his soul and shall be satisfied."[1]

What Mr. Toynbee eloquently affirms a few contemporaries of Jesus of Nazareth recognized. Jesus Christ was acknowledged to be the Son of God, uniquely and redemptively, by a few discern-

ing disciples in His own lifetime. His disgraceful death by legal
murder was followed by the cosmic response to His faith and love
and sacrifice which we know as the resurrection. In the power of
this total fact the first Christians went out to capture the world
for Christ. "Jesus is Lord!" was their battle slogan as they engaged in heroic spiritual warfare. "Remember Jesus Christ, crucified, risen, alive in His Body the Church!" was their rallying cry.
This is the faith tremendous, and this high and holy confidence
who can scorn who knows anything of subsequent history? Is it
any wonder that a mighty Russian thinker, Berdyaev, asserted
dogmatically, "The true starting point of Christianity is neither
God nor man, but the God who was made man; whom we know
not because we found Him, but because He found us, 'gathered
us by the power of His Spirit into the one great fellowship of His
Son.'" "God was in Christ reconciling the world to Himself,"
adjusting those living persons within His world to the supreme
reality—God Himself—from whom by folly, moral failure and
deep despair they had estranged themselves. It is tremendous, is it
not? Are you surprised that when we try to express it in anything
like coherent systematic fashion we trip over our logic, stumble
over our words, soar into abstractions, or get bogged down in
paradoxes? In divinity as in love what is best worth saying cannot
be said; God has said it in the Word made flesh in whom we behold His glory. When men and women like ourselves are confronted by this fact of history and of experience they end up on
their knees. Our confession cannot be other than that made by
one who had his intellectual difficulties swept aside by direct
encounter: "My Lord and my God!"[2]

If you think because of a kind of an allergy to orthodoxy that
you can escape this claim by blaming St. Paul for turning the
simple idyllic tale of a Palestinian teacher into a metaphysic and
a theology, you ought to be disabused of that notion! Paul made
articulate the inevitable truth experienced by himself and his
colleagues; truth confirmed in the experience of millions of un-

deluded persons since. No, the more visible satellite has not eclipsed the central Sun.

Here then is basic Christianity: *it is acknowledgment of the truth and commitment to the Person of Jesus Christ.* It is faith in the God who "in many and various ways spoke of old to our fathers by the prophets; but in these last days He has spoken to us by a Son, whom He appointed the heir of all things. . . . He reflects the glory of God and bears the very stamp of His nature, upholding the universe by His word of power."[3] Neither you nor I invented this, nor do we think that any group of men contrived it. The total event of the Lord Jesus Christ—His birth, His life and teachings, His mighty deeds, His sacrificial death and God's response to it in the resurrection, and His abiding presence within the community of His Spirit which we call the Church—this fact and our response to it is the heart of Christianity. A magazine reported a distinguished scientist's comment when he advocated increased exchange of students between nations to extend international understanding. "The best way to export an idea is to wrap it up in a person." When we reflect upon the incarnation of the Son of God, we feel that God Himself knew that if we were ever to grasp the idea of His holy, righteous and loving character and purpose He must "wrap it up" in a person. So the divine idea "became flesh and dwelt among us, full of grace and truth; we have beheld His glory, glory as of the only Son of the Father."[4] Through the eyes of faith we do behold Him.

> 'Tis the weakness in flesh that I cry for! my flesh, that I seek
> In the Godhead! I seek and I find it. O Saul, it shall be
> A Face like my face that receives thee; a Man like to me,
> Thou shalt love and be loved by forever: a Hand like this hand
> Shall throw open the gates of new life to thee! See the Christ
> stand![5]

Granted that this is a tremendous claim, that to skeptical minds it may prove what a friendly interpreter of the Faith called "the absurdity of Christianity," what difference does it make? After all, we do live in this modern age, and the concepts and categories

of a far-off era may be irrelevant to our need. Have not many
bridges across which other souls walked flowed down the river of
thought since Jesus lived "beneath the Syrian blue"? We do not
wish to give hospitality to venerable dogma if it is only to become
a bedridden veteran in the dormitory of the soul.

Here is the first difference made by acceptance of this basic
claim of Christianity: *because God was in Christ we can make
sense of the mysteries of our existence.* By God's revelation of
Himself in Christ we gain assurance that One who is perfect, holy
Love is actively operating here. Not all Christian thinkers would
go as far as Robert Browning in saying that

> the acknowledgment of God in Christ
> Accepted by thy reason, solves for thee
> All questions in the world and out of it.[6]

But all would agree that "the acknowledgment of God in Christ,
accepted by thy reason" and "lived into" by the total self in the
community of fellow believers, solves the main question. Is this
universe going it blind, or is it, despite factors to the contrary,
our Father's home? For the person who accepts basic Christianity
the latter reading is preponderantly convincing. Without the interpretation furnished by the Christian faith, life remains ambiguous. Once, painting a summer cottage, a teenager in our family
discovered that he could finish the job by using his left hand in
addition to his right. Proud of his achievement he announced,
"This makes me ambiguous!" Ambidextrous we may be, ambiguous our human situation and the mysterious universe assuredly
are to the person without the Faith. Christ is the key to the riddle.
As Alice Meynell wrote:

> With this ambiguous earth
> His dealings have been told us. These abide:
> The signal to a maid, the human birth,
> The lesson and the young man crucified.[7]

Dean Willard L. Sperry of Harvard puts the alternatives sharply:
"Either one of two things is true; either life is 'a tale told by an

idiot, full of sound and fury, signifying nothing,' or else the character of Jesus is a clue to reality."[8] Is it too much to expect that the Supreme Intelligence behind and through all things would not leave us in the dark concerning the meaning of it all? Surely, if He deserves the name of God and the homage of His creatures He would disclose something of the pattern of life, give enough light in the darkness for us to walk by. This the Christian witness declares He has done in Jesus Christ. In other religions much help is given; in Christ the partial becomes complete. He is the authentic voice and deed of the infinite and eternal God. "God was in Christ" and we find meaning and purpose in "this ambiguous earth."

He that sees Christ sees the Father, receives assurance that the heart of the Eternal "is most wonderfully kind," and righteous. Even more than this is needed if we are to know the kind of life to which eternity is promised. Deliverance from our worst enemies we must win or have won for us. Such *deliverance has been made,* says the Christian gospel, *and we can share in it.* Paul's testimony went beyond the declaration of the tremendous fact that "God was in Christ." "God was in Christ reconciling the world to Himself not counting their trespasses against them, and entrusting to us the message of reconciliation." It may be true that modern men are not worrying about their sins in the sense in which their ancestors did. But there persists a deep uneasiness, a profound and disintegrating sense of anxiety. Is a sense of guilt unknown to emancipated moderns? How often a physician of the soul confirms our own suspicion that we are sick, are under the power of death as far as our faith in life and our hope for tomorrow are concerned. In Jesus God provided the antidote. For our despair He gives hope, for our sense of guilt He offers forgiveness, for our inner hurt and loneliness the healing and friendship of His love. Something transpired in Palestine nineteen centuries ago in the life, death and resurrection of Christ that makes it possible for you and me to come into the presence of the Most High God just

as we are and to receive from Him the pardon and peace we
desperately need. So it is that the Cross and the resurrection
achieved the victory of God over our chief enemies, sin and death.
We are saved as we are reconciled with the great God who made
us and loves us and delivers us from the power of sin and death.
As we repent, change our minds and place our lives in His hands
to be changed, we are forgiven. For our deep disease of will and
emotions we are given health. A homespun testimony by a member of Alcoholics Anonymous may make this glorious fact clear.
He was telling his fellow members of his moral defeat and victory.
Once, he recalled, he had wanted to buy an unusually fine watch.
It combined a chronometer, a stop watch, and a few of the features of a calendar and astronomical observatory; it indicated the
day of the month and the phases of the moon. "In fact all it
lacked was hot and cold running water." He realized that if it
ever needed repair it could not be taken to an ordinary repair-
man. It would need to be taken to its maker. "Then one day," he
said, "it came to me that my life was a very complicated affair
like that watch. It had broken down, and was running out of control. I decided that my only chance was to take it back to its
Maker." "Come after Me," said the Lord to Peter, "and I will
make you." Come to Me, says the living Lord to every complicated and broken person today, "and I will remake you." By the
operation of the divine Spirit, the redemptive action of the Maker
of men is available to every soul. "God was in Christ reconciling
the world to Himself, not counting their trespasses against them,
and entrusting to us the message of reconciliation." "Therefore,
if any one is in Christ, he is a new creation; the old has passed
away, behold, the new has come."[9]

What difference does Christ make? Accepted, trusted, obeyed,
He provides a transcript to reality, supplies meaning to an otherwise ambiguous existence; He saves us from our spiritual enemies
and makes us more than conquerors. He is the Truth we most
need to know and act upon. He is our Saviour because in Him

God enters our life with His forgiveness and help. More than this we find as we commit ourselves to the God we know in Him. *Christ becomes an abiding presence on every road we take.* The living Lord is the Holy Spirit in intimate, divine-and-human terms. There is not where He is not. Did He not promise, "I am with you always, to the close of the age"[10] and beyond? Whatever may be true for other creeds the Christian belief in Christ is more than intellectual acceptance of the noblest hypothesis; it is personal trust in an unseen but present Companion and Guide. As we proceed to fulfill the tasks He appoints for our time; as we seek to do His will, and maintain through private and public worship our contact with Him, we know that we go on our way attended by the unfailing Friend and invincible Lord. A vivid sense of His nearness may not be ours at every stage of our journey, but He will be near. The vision may fade, but not He. A wartime chaplain told me of a young soldier he knew whose captain showed rare understanding of the boy's fear of being afraid in a critical situation. After he had completed his first sentry duty uncomfortably near enemy lines, the young fellow started to crawl back to his own company's position. He was filled with grateful wonder that he had been able to stay at his post without panic. He had moved only a few yards when he was startled to see his captain near him. "I've been here right along," said the fatherly officer. Have we not made similar discovery of the reinforcing presence of our beloved Captain? As a man who practiced Christ's presence once said: "It is a great satisfaction to have one standing by to keep you at your best."

> I have a Captain, and the heart
> Of every private man
> Has drunk in valour from His eyes
> Since first the war began;
> He is most merciful in fight,
> And of His scars a single sight
> The embers of our failing might
> Into a flame can fan.[11]

He keeps us at our best. He empowers us to help others to be their best too. Will you test this basic truth by making Him the basis of your life?

PRAYER: *O Lord Jesus Christ, whom having not seen save with the eyes of faith we love, men and women in every age and land have found Thee to be the Way, the Truth, and the Life. We acknowledge Thee to be the Lord. Take thy power and reign. Through us and through the blessed company of Thy faithful followers everywhere fulfill Thy purpose that all may live in newness of life; for Thy kingdom's sake and for the glory of God the Father with whom and with the Holy Spirit Thou dost live eternally, one God blessed for ever. Amen.*

2

Good News for "Nobodies"

. . . as servants of God we commend ourselves in every way: . . . as unknown, and yet well known. . . .   2 CORINTHIANS 6:4, 9

Called "nobodies" we must be in the public eye. 2 CORINTHIANS 6:9 (Phillips)

ONE of the enemies of effective Christian living is the feeling that we do not matter much in the scheme of things. Just because we are human we deeply desire to be loved, to be reasonably secure, and to feel significant. When these demands are denied, life sags, and we limp through our days instead of marching to brave music. An investigation among college students showed that 90 per cent of a fairly large sampling were afflicted with the feeling of insignificance.

Much mediocre behavior, and not a little that is worse, may be due to this opinion that we do not count, that what we are and what we do does not matter. Good that needs assistance suffers, wrong that cries for resistance goes unopposed because so many of us accept a low evaluation of ourselves and of our contributions.

True, there may be a delicious sense of relief in assuming that as far as headlines, society columns and executive committees are concerned, we are "nobodies." Who wants to live in a goldfish bowl? Who envies the prominent citizen who may be investigated either by the department of internal revenue or a congressional committee? Let the fierce glare of publicity beat on other heads! So Emily Dickinson sought to make herself invulnerable by an attitude she celebrated in her whimsical lines:

I'm nobody! Who are you?
  Are you nobody, too?
Then there's a pair of us—don't tell!
  They'd banish us, you know!

How dreary to be somebody!
  How public, like a frog
To tell your name the livelong day
  To an admiring bog![1]

And yet! You and I need a healthy sense of our own significance if we are to make the most of our best for our own sake as well as for the sake of others. In spite of factors which conspire to make us feel unimportant, we respond to recognition, to approval, to the opinion of respected persons that we are needed, as morning glories open to the sun. An amusing example was provided by an English cartoonist. He depicted a mild-looking man looking at his picture in a newspaper advertisement. This British counterpart of Caspar Milquetoast had sent in an endorsement of a patent medicine. The manufacturer had obtained his photograph and printed it along with the customer's unsolicited testimonial. As the man studies this visible proof of his publicity value he says, "Is this fame or only a passing wave of popularity?" The fact remains, as Gilbert K. Chesterton observed, that "the crimes of the Devil who thinks himself of immeasurable value are as nothing to the crimes of the Devil who thinks himself of no value."

If you and I are wrestling with this particular demon who uses many wiles to convince us that we are of no value, what should be our strategy?

The apostle Paul would not receive many requests that he submit his biography to "Who's Who," nor is it likely that he would be nominated in his lifetime for a place in a Hall of Fame. Nevertheless, he was sure that as servants of God we must seek "to commend ourselves in every way . . . as unknown and yet well known." Even when we are "called 'nobodies' we must be in the public eye."

Who can help us attain a healthy sense of our true significance? Christ can! He is able to make us more than conquerors over this foe of our usefulness and joy.

How does Christ help us to replace the debilitating mood which persuades us that when we are called "nobodies" we are accurately named?

Christ helps us first and chiefly by revealing that "behind the dim unknown standeth God within the shadow." He not only keeps watch above His own—the obscure "little people," as well as those occupying the seats of the mighty; He loves the least and the lowest of His human family. The total fact of the Lord Jesus Christ demonstrates this liberating truth that you and I matter to God, and matter tremendously. The human life of God's beloved Son, His teaching, His deeds of healing, all prove the divine concern, the indescribably high estimate He places on us. Supremely, the sacrificial death on the Cross "for us men and for our salvation" shows what God Himself thinks of us. "Why, one will hardly die for a righteous man—though perhaps for a good man one will dare even to die." Perhaps for a distinguished, eminently useful leader another will give his life. "But God shows His love for us in that while we were yet sinners [and very commonplace sinners at that] Christ died for us."[2]

Have you had dark moments when you asked petulantly, or angrily, as the writer of the thirteenth Psalm asked, "How long wilt thou forget me, O God, for ever?" Were you quiet long enough to hear the divine answer: "Yet even were a mother to forget her child, yet will I not forget thee"? Once on a visit to Scotland I came to the Isle of Whithorn, one of the cradles of British Christianity. In the kirkyard are many ancient tombstones, centuries old. One interested me more than others. Almost swallowed by the earth, the marker's inscription at the top remained legible. It was this: "YOU THINK I'M FORGOT. BUT I'M NOT!" Who did he think he was fooling? His name was obliterated; had it not been who would have known anything about him? Yet he was no silly egotist, for he and his loved ones knew that "in Christ" a man is loved and known forever.

"Are not five sparrows sold for two pennies?" asked Jesus. "And not one of them is forgotten before God. . . . Fear not; you are of more value than many sparrows."[3] In spite of my weakness and sinning and being a "nobody" in the eyes of the world, He must consider me worth something, muses Paul: He loved me and gave Himself for me. If you feel forgotten by God and man, could it be that you have forgotten God? Christ knew what it was to walk in the crowded loneliness of a city. Always He knew that He was never less alone than when He seemed alone, deserted, forgotten. "Yet I am not alone, for the Father is with me."[4]

Take a long look at the way you have come. Are there not tokens, evidences of a Love that remembers, that never forgets or fails or lets us go? Over against the hurts and deprivations which seem to prove that you are nobody as far as God and your fellows are concerned, put down those experiences which increased your sense of significance. Above all, keep steadily in sight our blessed Lord who came that we might find life meaningful and splendid in the friendship and service of God. Where His friendship is, we can travel on without self-pity. Because of God's love in Christ we can prove ourselves God's servants "as unknown and yet well known."

Flowing out of this knowledge of God and of His personal love toward the least of us, *we become "somebody" in the only society worth joining.* God in Christ saves us from a low opinion of ourselves as He does from the other sins which so easily pull us down, by setting us to follow Him in the tasks He sets for our time. We are saved to serve. We serve by linking our little lives with the divine society, the community of the Holy Spirit, which seeks to make God's rule prevail in every relationship. How significant we feel when we lose ourselves in a cause to which the future belongs!

Wendell Phillips' prescription for the young man who asked

the veteran reformer how he could make his life count remains valid: "Find a great cause and grow strong in its service." If you seek such a cause, look around you. The Christian Church where we live offers us opportunities and needs our help. As Christians we belong to the great and good cause of the Kingdom of God. However limited our abilities, however meager the resources we think are ours, each of us has at least one talent. The Lord still works His miracle, still multiplies the handful of loaves and fishes we put at His disposal. Face to face with global tragedy, wide-scale political inertia and corruption, discrimination against minority groups, how easy it is to evade what we can do by asking "Why don't *they*—the leaders, the important people—do something?" Yet "they" commonly move in response to the organized, intelligent prodding of "ordinary people." To belong to what Elton Trueblood calls "the fellowship of the concerned" is to belong to the company of men and women who know that they have passed from death to life constructive and thrilling because they love the brethren. When Mr. William E. Gladstone was Prime Minister of Great Britain he was asked why he attended church so faithfully. It could not be because he enjoyed the music, or found the sermons uniformly inspiring. "I go to church," said the Victorian statesman, "because I love England." So you and I might say, "I go to church and through the church and other agencies to serve, to engage in study and action because I love America, and that 'other country,' the Kingdom of God on earth."

In recent years a week in March offers us "One Great Hour of Sharing." In this hour we share a little of our plenty with others around the earth whose need is desperate. You and I may not have much to give. Shall we then excuse ourselves? My Scottish mother often quoted the old saying "many mickles mak' a muckle." Many littles make much. Around five million persons are in desperate need in Korea. Aid in 1951 reached only one in ten. We can do better than that if more of us give more of our "mickles" (not to be confused with "nickles")—the clothing and the dollars we can spare. Of course the Christian motive behind such gifts is more than the feeling of significance which accompanies a charitable act. We give because we have been given so much. Where need calls, the voice of Christ is heard. Where need is met the Lord of life is served.

In practical helpfulness to the beaten and broken, the hungry and the forsaken, we are content to be unknown, as long as the compassion of Christ's people is well known to those who need it most.

Shoulder to shoulder with comrades of Christ where we are, and through the fellowship of His universal Church with co-workers everywhere, we stand up and are counted. As we witness to His supremacy, as by His Spirit's aid we seek to enthrone Him in every province of His dominion, we find that we are "unknown yet well known." In the ongoing Christian movement we are "somebody." We commend ourselves as God's servants, "as unknown yet well known" because we are within the Body of Christ.

As we live in God and in His high opinion of us, as we lose ourselves in the divine society and service for the sake of Christ, we cease belittling ourselves and recover a sense of significance. This further grace is given us: *we become willing to be among the unpublicized disciples of our Master.*

It does take grace to go without recognition, but this grace the Lord supplies. In His company we attain even this degree of maturity that we are willing to be among the world's anonymous helpers. Has it ever occurred to you how much we owe to that large company whose nom de plume is "Anonymous"? When I was a boy, the only reading permitted during church service was the Bible or hymnbook. As a hymnbook was always available and more attractively printed, I read it more frequently than the Scriptures. I was impressed by the prodigious work of a gentleman named "Anon." Who wrote *Te Deum Laudamus? Adeste Fideles?* Turning to the classics of our faith, who wrote many of the Psalms? (Like Alexander Whyte, the Scottish minister, when a younger colleague strove to enlighten him concerning the multiple authorship of the Psalms, you may say, "David will do for me.") Who wrote the Book of Job? the Epistle to the Hebrews? Who knows? Does it matter? They are "unknown yet well known." Who made our miracle drugs of modern medicine possible? Do we know the names of all who shared in the research and experiment? Once in Dundee, Scotland, Signor Marconi paid tribute to a man who had made his achievements in wireless and radio possible. He was unknown by name. "Without that man of genius," said Marconi, "my work would have been impossible." What was the name of the good Samaritan?

Your work and mine may seem trivial. But our fidelity is not trivial. Our witness to whatsoever things are true, honorable, just, pure, lovely and gracious is not trivial. Who holds the fabric of society together? For the most part just unknown, decent, responsible men and women, who commend themselves as servants of God and soldiers of the common good as "unknown and yet well known." These are they who demonstrate the livableness of life and the worth of Christlike standards. How could we enjoy the measure of ordered freedom and abundant life that is ours without

> the unknown good that rest
> In God's still memory, folded deep;
> The bravely dumb that did their deed,
> And scorned to blot it with a name,
> Men of the plain heroic breed
> That loved Heaven's silence more than fame.[5]

Christ never promised fame or adulation to those who follow Him. In the nature of things, the Christian's true life is unspectacular and out of the sight of men. Interior discipline and intercession through prayer, the daily battle for the highest, and the bearing of the Cross, are not for any but God to see. The Christian's is a life "hid with Christ in God." But other lives are affected for good, how much who can measure?

Maturity attests itself as we become content to play as competently as we can a humble part in life's orchestra. Most of us begin, and some of us continue, determined to play only solo parts. As we grow in the grace of Christ we grow in wisdom, and find durable satisfaction in having even a small part in producing the Lord's New World Symphony. A story is told of Arturo Toscanini and his rehearsal of the New York Philharmonic Orchestra in Beethoven's Ninth Symphony. If it is apocryphal it deserves to be true. Each group of instrumentalists played its part alone. When the Maestro judged that all were ready, he had them play the entire work without interruption. The fire in the conductor's soul touched each player. When the finale reached its stirring close, there was silence. One violinist whispered to a colleague, "If he scolds us after such playing I'll push him over into the pit!" But the master did not scold. "Who am I?" he asked. "Who is Toscanini? I am nobody. Who are you? You are nobody." He paused for a moment. Then with face glowing he exclaimed, "It is Beethoven—he is everything!" In the realm of music it is true. To a Christian, a similar question comes: Who am I? Who are you? We are nobody. Christ is everything! His communication of God's love, His kind of living, His quality of character in personality and in community: Christ is everything. To be known of Him is enough.

PRAYER: *Accept our thanks, O Lord, that thou dost restore our self-respect. Give us grace to fulfill patiently and gladly whatever duty Thou appointest, doing small things in the day of small things, and great labors if thou summonest us to any. Teach us to serve Thee and not to ask for any reward save that of knowing that we do Thy will; through Jesus Christ our Lord. Amen.*

3
How Can a Man Know God?

Oh that I knew where I might find Him!   JOB 23:3

I have heard of Thee by the hearing of the ear: but now mine eye seeth Thee.   JOB 42:5

AT A BOYS' camp on the shores of a northern Canadian lake a discussion on religion led one staff member to ask privately one of the most significant questions any human being can ask. "I can understand how a person can believe in God," he said. "Where I can't follow you is when you say a person can *know* God. How can a man know God?" To this thoughtful young man, a war veteran preparing himself for a career as physician, the question was not academic. He had pondered the plight of man sufficiently to realize that loss of vital faith was a contributing factor to that plight. He knew, as another said, that "to give up faith in the Other that is more than man is to become less than man." Moreover, he personally desired to know God as a present reality in his own experience. He was agnostic only because firsthand acquaintance with deity seemed to him to be impossible. Like Job under stress, his query and subsequent conversation revealed one who was saying in modern speech, "Oh that I knew where I might find Him!" But his mind balked at the assumption that a puny inhabitant of a tiny plant could know the Creative Mind and Spirit that is over and above as well as within worlds and systems. He wanted to believe in God not only from the top of his mind but from the bottom of his heart. He would give much, he said, to be able to repeat meaningfully Job's later affirmation, "I had heard of Thee with the hearing of the ear, but now mine eye seeth Thee."

How can a man know God? This question is not dreamed up by the preacher. Much more prevalent than downright atheism or the practical atheism of nominally religious people is the reluctant agnosticism of thoughtful, respectable persons. Such individuals long to know God other than by hearsay, but they fear self-deception. Unless we are mystics with a highly developed intuitional grasp of the unseen Companion of our spirits, or have had rich experience of His reality, the question is for us too. How can we know God so that He is the realest fact in the universe and the infinite factor in our lives which makes all the difference?

Imagine yourself along with me talking the matter over with the earnest young seeker. What would you say to him? You might begin by assuring him that any seeker who is seriously in quest of firsthand knowledge of God may become a finder. Spiritual experience is not reserved for exceptional persons. Any human being with normal equipment regardless of temperament or intelligence quotient may know the Father. Spiritual babes may find God revealed to them when wise and prudent minds find Him hidden. It would be wise, too, to remind him that there is more than one pathway to the Presence of God. Did not the seer on Patmos who left us his book of the Revelation discover that there are twelve gates leading to the City of God?[1] Rightly we distrust the man who says concerning a particular approach or experience, "This is the only way to find God or to be found by Him." An airlines pilot may prefer one "beam" to another, but he knows that there are other routes he may travel with confidence.

Here are roads down which other honest seekers have encountered God in firsthand experience. One guidepost tells us to *look for God on all levels of human life and activity*. Perversely we are tempted to think we can get on the track only if we follow the road which otherworldly saints have marked "spiritual." To be sure, one of the tested ways to receive knowledge of God's reality and personal dealings with us is to share with others in the mysterious and wonderful experience of worship. Why should we not explore the possibilities of the Church which despite its imperfections is the one Society keeping the light of God before the eyes of men? By its history and in its worship does it not exist to perpetuate and to offer to men and women a way to God? A remarkable poem has come down to us from a man who was depressed and desperate because of the conditions of his society. As he surveyed his contemporary world, God seemed absent or at least impotent. Then he went to church. The ancient temple he entered was not very different from our temples of faith and worship today. Within that sanctuary something happened to him and in him. He gained new perspective on the old facts. He was given the assurance he most needed. You can read the account in the seventy-third Psalm. This was his finding:

> Yet I am always beside Thee;
> Thou holdest my right hand,
> guiding me with thy counsel . . .
> Body and soul may fail,
> But God my strength is mine,
> mine own for evermore.[2]

Men and women who join themselves to other seekers and finders in the community of Christ at worship frequently receive similar authentic evidence of God's sustaining and guiding wisdom and care. We cannot separate His Spirit from His Body the Church. Yet the infinite Spirit who cannot be confined to buildings made by men's hands is at work in many other places and situations. Is He not at work in the operating rooms of hospitals where dedicated men and women act consciously or unconsciously as His instruments of healing? Is He not the inspiration and the answer of trained and dedicated minds seeking to discover new and better ways for human beings to live and work together? Shall we not find Him where parents lovingly and wisely encourage the growth of their children in maturity? Can the vast wisdom and love which is God not be discerned in the sacrificial struggles of men and women on behalf of a more abundant life for their fellows? James Russell Lowell was sure that God is in all that lifts and liberates the human spirit, and we may be sure too. In all that contributes to the creation of a world community of fraternal righteousness and just peace He moves and inspires. In the honest craftsman, artist and artisan; in the faithful worker in humble and in high places; in the common relationships of everyday living, the Spirit of the Most High may be experienced. Look for Him among His human helpers.

> I needs must meet Him, for He hath beset
> All roads that men do travel.

A second suggestion places a mirror in front of ourselves. This may be a disturbing exercise but it is a needful one. A newspaper writer asked the question, "What sort of a mirror have you?" He urged readers to acquire an enlarging mirror—the kind that shows up the details, good or bad, of one's countenance. Take care also, he added, that the light shines on your face. When we look at ourselves, or rather, when we look within ourselves, what do we see? Once in conversation with a prosperous young man, Jesus held up an "enlarging mirror" to him.[3] He helped the young fellow to see that within himself was the chief obstacle to the kind of spiritual satisfactions he sought. The rich young ruler was unwilling to obey the high ethical demands of great religion. Could it be that God is unreal, and religion irrelevant to us because we have not faced up to our own inward condition? It is possible that our religious difficulty is moral rather than intellectual. "Who is the god of the Christians?" asked an arrogant pagan of his Christian prisoner. The reply he made is pertinent: "If thou art worthy thou shalt know." No man can be morally perfect, but every man must be honest and humble in acknowledging personal weakness. God is related to man not chiefly as the almighty Creator to His creature, nor as the First Cause to the thinker, but as the Saviour to the lost. It is when we expose ourselves to the light of God which shines through Christ that we know we are lost; that we do not know where we are or where we should be going. In our encounter with God's holy love we realize most acutely that something is wrong in our thinking, in our habitual attitudes and actions. Then we find ourselves as our evangelical predecessors would have said, "under judgment." We find courage and insight to confess, "I am part of the social problem; I am the problem of racial prejudice. I am part of the problem of war. I am the man who knows His judgment and must receive His mercy." This is what Christians have meant when they have said that we can find God in the Cross. He is the God who judges and reveals, and reveals Himself as the one who destroys the evil and forgives the evildoer. *You can find God as you come to know yourself in your weakness and failure, and as you turn to Him for deliverance and peace.* He comes today as long ago to seek and to save that which is lost.

Here is a third signpost on the road to knowledge of God: *you may know Him as you move out naturally and persistently to cultivate His friendship.* Is not this the way we come to know another human person? We go where he is, share his thoughts and plans, work with him and play with him. How do you keep friendship in repair? By frequent conversation with your friend. But do we human beings ever know another until, as we say, he "unburdens" himself to us? John Donne's statement that "no man is an Island, entire of itself" is true, but only self-revelation through intimate communion reveals that each man is "a piece of the Continent." It is not otherwise with the supreme Person. If our knowledge of God depended solely on our discovery of God our quest would be futile. He must take the initiative, He must unburden or reveal His heart to us. The exciting claim of the Christian faith is that He has and does! Our discovery is the human side of His self-revelation. He reveals Himself in the world He has made and is making, in the pattern of history, in good men and women, in beauty and goodness and truth. Is this all? Is this enough? No, for we are persons and He must reveal Himself in terms we can grasp. So, "in the fullness of time," at the decisive moment, the infinite and eternal took human form. Someone said beautifully that the incarnation of God in Jesus Christ is God taking little short steps so that we His children could keep up with Him. "The Word became flesh and dwelt among us, and we beheld *His* glory. . . . No one has ever seen God; the only Son, who is in the bosom of the Father, He has made Him known."4 "For it is the God who said, 'Let light shine out of darkness,' who has shone in our hearts to give the light of the knowledge of the glory of God in the face of Christ."5

Do you say, yes, but how can even the best personality who lived nineteen hundred years ago enable us to know God in this year of perplexity? The answer is this: As Jesus was in the days of His human life, so God is eternally. Keep Christ steadily in sight. By an act of imaginative faith, picture Him before you. He will step out of the pages of the New Testament and make Himself known. Act on the insights which come to you from contemplation of His words and deeds. Go into your daily task as you think He would go if He had been sent to your place. Keep open the lines of communication with His Spirit through daily meditation, prayer, and through faithful participation in worship. Do those things which you believe to be most nearly in accord with His purpose. Join Him as He proceeds in every situation to overcome evil with good. We learn to know God by living with Him, and by doing those things which He desires. In order to know, said Jesus, we must act. "If any man's will is to do His will, he shall know."6 Verification is by commitment.

To the question, Can a man know God? God Himself answers in a glorious affirmative. Christ is the Yes of God to our question. Prophets, saints and martyrs, together with an immense company of ordinary men and women like ourselves, unite in exultant confirmation. How can a man know God? Let us gather up the simple directions which have helped seekers to become happy finders.

First, look for God on all the levels of life. Remember that on these levels is the Church to be explored, and its worship to be experienced.

Second, face yourself in your weakness as in your strength, letting the light of God in Christ expose any moral barrier you have built against His coming. If your heart condemns you, as it is likely to do, remember that God is greater than your heart, in judgment and also in mercy. Give yourself as well as your failures and deficiencies to Him. Victory on this battlefield comes through surrender. Realize His forgiveness, and trust His resources for every future testing.

Third, cultivate His friendship. The means of such cultivation the Church calls "the means of grace"—aids whereby His loving help becomes available to us. Familiarize yourself with the Gospels, and learn what God meant to Jesus and through Jesus to His first followers. Live your way into His friendship. Maintain communication with Him through prayer and worship. Every day "tune in" to your headquarters.

Fourth, live in terms of Christlike love, relying upon His unfailing strength to keep you from falling into the old selfish ways. "God is love, and he who abides in love abides in God, and God abides in him."[7] Selfishness insulates us from God. To Jesus God was near because He lived habitually with unconquerable friendliness, and with unbreakable love toward the least and lowest as well as toward those who were privileged and powerful. God is more than a personal satisfaction to be enjoyed; He is love to be shared.

Remember always that we would not seek Him had He not first sought us, that we could not love Him had He not first loved us. As a saintly woman said in her old age to the man who had loved her in her youth, "The mystery plays fair." *He* whose mystery no man can fathom "plays fair": "He is a rewarder of them that diligently seek Him."[8] "He who has My commandments and keeps them, he it is who loves Me; and he who loves Me will be loved by My Father, and I will love Him and manifest Myself to him."[9] He will manifest Himself, will make Himself

known, as we commit ourselves to all that we know of God in
Christ. As we follow Him along the way we take in obedience
to His Spirit, He will meet us. We shall arrive

> Where ask is have, where seek is find,
> Where knock is open wide.

Do you ask, But what do we do to start? Is there not something
we ought to do, other than what we have talked about? From
Great Britain comes a story which gives the Christian answer.
A fine Christian couple, denied natural parenthood, successfully
applied for the adoption of a little girl. This particular child
had been cruelly rejected by her own parents, and in other ways
had learned to distrust grownups. At last the day came when the
foster mother arrived at the placement home. The matron
ushered the little girl into the presence of her new friend. "I
have come to take you to your new home," said the kindly
woman. "You will have your own room, with your own bed, and
chairs, and your own clothes and playthings. It will be your very
own home, and my husband and I will be your own parents."
Suspiciously the little girl asked, "What do I have to do for all
this?" Realizing the cruel experience of life which prompted this
question, the woman came down to the level of the child's eyes,
and tenderly said to her. "Why, my dear, you don't have to do
anything. All you need to do is to try to love me and to be my
child." What do you have to do for the knowledge and love of
God which He offers you? God who draws near to us through
the life and cross and living presence of the Lord Jesus whispers:
"You do not need to do anything. You cannot do anything. All
you need to do is to try to love Me and be My child."

PRAYER: *Do Thou teach us, O God our Father, that all hearts
are empty except Thou fillest them, and all desires fail except
they yearn for Thee. Of Thy compassion do Thou give us grace
to seek Thee. Nay, rather, do Thou find us as we are that we may
be Thine and Thou mayest be ours forever; in Jesus Christ, Thy
Son, our Lord. Amen.*

4

Wake Up and Live

Why all this stress on behaviour? Because, as I think you have realised, the present time is of the highest importance—it is time to wake up to reality. Every day brings God's salvation nearer.   Romans 13:11 (Phillips)

WHEN I was a junior sky pilot—student minister of a mission field in the Canadian northwest—an unusual advertisement by a small railway company appeared in a newspaper. "Wanted:" it announced, "three hundred sleepers in good condition." One discouraged pastor was reported to have written the advertiser offering his entire congregation. Personal temptation to do likewise was easily resisted, but I was disturbed by the habit of one of my most loyal parishioners. He would settle into an audibly enjoyable sleep at the close of the hymn preceding the sermon. With friendly frankness he assured me the cause was physical, not homiletical. Subsequently during an urban pastorate a similar situation presented itself Sunday by Sunday. An elderly gentleman of culture and piety closed his eyes, nodded, and relaxed into apparently profound slumber shortly after the sermon began. Until I knew my friend's personal difficulty in keeping awake in any comfortable environment, I was tempted to repeat the late Dr. John A. Hutton's appeal: "There is a brother here who is not playing fair with the preacher. Before the text has been announced he is settling down for a nap. I appeal to his sportmanship to play fair and start from scratch. Let him at least remain awake long enough to hear the text. Thereafter if he goes to sleep it will be the preacher's fault."

Much more serious is the somnolence of good people concerning live issues, basic values and virtues. Alert to much that is

39

going on in the visible world around them, they act as sleep-walkers as far as awareness of critical issues of time and eternity are concerned. To them comes the Advent warning:

> The present time is of the highest importance—it is time to wake up to reality.

St. Paul in this section of his letter to the Romans appeals to the sense of crisis as a motive to live with ethical and spiritual seriousness. As our New Testament scholars remind us, the epistles plainly show that the early Church lived in a climate of crisis: a New Age was breaking in upon them. Paul's fellow Christians were living as if the Kingdom of God had already come, as indeed for those commited to Christ it had come. But there were others, for whom the fading of a sense of an imminent Day of the Lord lulled them into a false and spiritually dangerous apathy. Hence, the apostle's insistence that every day is a day of Crisis for the Christian, with God Himself pressing disturbingly upon His world: "—it is time to wake up to reality. Every day brings God's salvation nearer. The night is nearly over, the Day has almost dawned. Let us fling away the things that men do in the dark, and let us arm ourselves for the fight of the Day! Let us live cleanly, as in the daylight, not in the 'delights' of getting drunk, or playing with sex, nor yet in quarrelling or jealousies. Let us be Christ's men from head to foot. . . ."[1]

Is this not an authentic word for us and for our contemporaries? To be sure, we grow weary of constant challenges to renewed effort. When social critics and political experts shout continuously of one recurring crisis after another we tune in another station or read a less clamorous publication. No one enjoys even a competent and prophetic interpreter of current trends who writes as one able woman correspondent has been accused of doing, at the top of her voice. It is also true that the human soul in times of tension may need to sing something less strenuous than "Awake my soul, stretch every nerve, And press with vigor on." Again and again we need to linger in quiet pastures by still

waters that God may restore our tattered souls. Nevertheless, the
trumpet call to wakefulness and action must be sounded if we
are to "arm ourselves for the fight of the Day." Those responsive
instruments of the divine Word whom we call the prophets had
no doubt about it. A trill on a sweet flute simply would not do
to play the Lord's song in a time of turmoil. "Set the trumpet
to thy mouth!" cries Hosea. Jeremiah repeats the same curt
command. Ezekiel reiterates it, and Isaiah, too. "It is time to
wake up to reality," to the reality of the holy and righteous God
who is marching on, to the reality of invasion by the foes of
goodness, truth and freedom, to the reality of ultimate victory
for invincible Love. "Can you not keep awake?" Christ asked His
disciples.

Does this emphasis seem exaggerated? Have you doubts as to
the necessity of blasting sleeping souls awake? Competent observers of the world situation are sure there is urgent need of waking
us up to the perils and opportunities confronting Western civilization at this hour. The best of them go further, saying that we
cannot deal effectively with the perils nor exploit greatly the
opportunities unless first of all we wake up to the supreme
reality of God's self-revelation in Jesus Christ. Does some friend
of youth suggest that at least the young men and young women
of our time need no such awakening? Was ever a generation more
awake, more keenly aware of the issues of life? Recall the seriousness with which war veterans pursued their studies in school
and college. Many of these were awake, maintained alertness, and
as a result prepared themselves for long-term service of significance. But these were, and are, exceptions, declare men who
know young people and like much of what they know. Here, for
example, is the distinguished British educationalist, Sir Walter
Moberly, writing in his searching analysis of higher education,
The Crisis in the University:[2]

> The cultural failure of the universities is seen in the stu-
> dents. In recent years large numbers of these have been
> apathetic and have had neither wide interests nor compelling

convictions. . . . Whatever the cause, the university today lives
and moves and has its being in a moral and cultural fog.

Sir Walter is convinced that we live in a time of exceptional
crisis. Ours is an era far more critical for survival of all that
matters to Western man than that of one hundred years ago. He
is persuaded also that in the last resort the issue depends chiefly
on the beliefs and sentiments of men. Yet the younger citizens
who ought to be concerned and who should include in their
concern a revitalized Christianity, are apathetic, spiritually
asleep. Writing in an issue of a popular illustrated magazine in
the autumn of 1950, Canon Bernard Iddings Bell makes a similar
indictment of American education. "Our public schools and
colleges are rarely anti-religious," he declared. "They simply
ignore religion. They look on it as a minor amusement . . . an
innocuous pastime preferred by a few to golf or Canasta." These
critics are Christian men, informed and careful in appraisal of
facts; they also know and love the institutions they analyze. Let
no one condemn our schools and colleges for this indifference to
religion unless he sees himself under like condemnation. For are
not students and youth generally part of the world we have made?
Do they not reflect their elders' attitudes and practices? We, too,
share their working philosophy and much of their way of living,
and like it.

As for churches and church folk would you say that we give
the impression of being excited about the truth we profess? That
we are eager to share the Good News with others everywhere, and
exhibit enthusiasm and resolution in practicing "the ethics of
Crisis"? One critic of organized Christianity asked sarcastically,
"Would you imagine Christianity to be the religion whose
Founder was said to have come to kindle a fire on the earth?"
To many on the outside looking in we must seem timid and tepid,
half believers in a casual creed. "It is time to wake up to reality.
Every day brings God's salvation—and God's judgment—nearer."
It is not that Christ asks or needs fiercely agitated followers; He
does seek and need men and women who are aware of their

responsibility to operate as a creative Christian minority in a pagan world. Christopher Fry, the English playwright, recently wrote a comedy with tragic overtones, entitled *The Lady's Not for Burning*.[3] Set in a medieval period, the drama portrays with ironic humor the plight of respectable people insensitive to the desperate condition of a victim of superstition. One of them, Margaret Devize, confesses that she finds it impossible "to be Christian in two directions at once." Thomas Mendip, a discharged soldier, and the most perceptive character in the story, tries to arouse her to the witch hunt proceeding in the nearby street:

> Oh, be disturbed,
> Be disturbed, madam, to the extent of a tut,
> And I will thank God for all civilization.
> This is my last throw, my last poor gamble
> On the human heart.

How God must be trying to say that to you and me and all others who acknowledge Him to be the Lord! In our church, in our community, in our homes, there is wrong to be resisted and righted, good causes desperately needing assistance—and we turn and toss in our sleep day after deadly day. Corruption in government flourishes unchallenged, racial discrimination works its hateful havoc, religious bigotry and irreligious paganism hurt and impoverish all infected by them. On our very street and on the streets of the world injustice and war defile and destroy countless lives.

> Oh, be disturbed,
> Be disturbed, comrade in Christ, to the extent of a tut,
> And many will thank God for Christian civilization.

Now hear and receive the Word of the Lord as it comes through His dauntless trumpeter, St. Paul: "Why all this stress on behaviour? Because, as I think you have realised, the present time is of the highest importance—it is time to wake up to reality. Every day brings God's salvation nearer."

To what are we to awake? To the meaning and the implications of God's salvation. What does this signify? This first and most: that God has visited and redeemed His people in the person of His Son Jesus Christ; that His revelation must effect a revolution in our total way of thinking and acting; that our response of obedient trust must be widened and deepened within the community of Christ, the Church. In loyalty to the Mind of Christ and by daily reliance on His enabling grace, we can work with other Christians in helping mankind find a way of life that will bring peace and justice, security and creative life to nations and to individual men and women.

Does our awakening and that of others depend on us alone? It would be palpably false to say that it does. On every highway of thought and toil there are signs visible to the eyes of faith telling us, "Danger: God at Work." Danger? Yes, proceed at your peril if you regard His world and His Church as a kind of private "Slumber Shop." Where the Spirit of God is at work there is life and power unlimited. It is for us to be His responsible instruments. Concerning John Knox it was said by an English ambassador in Edinburgh that his voice "is able in one hour to putt more lyf in us than fyve hundred trumpets continually blustering at once in our ears." Whatever you say of that dour and dauntless Scottish reformer you cannot say his were somnambulant sermons. By your witness and work, by your own winged alertness to the needs of your place and time and the resources in Christ to meet those needs, you, too, can put life into men's souls. Does it seem ludicrous and absurd to picture yourself blowing martial blasts on a trumpet? At least you and I can keep awake, can hear what God the Lord has to say to His people. At least you can wake up to the tremendous fact of Christ, and the imperious call to serve Him which the Spirit ever sounds.

In his report of the Transfiguration experience, St. Luke included a detail loaded with relevant and luminous truth for us as we enter into the season and meaning of Advent: "Peter and they that were with him were heavy with sleep; *and when they were fully awake, they saw His glory*"[14] . . . *and their duty.*

PRAYER: *O God who art both the author of peace and the disturber of conscience, save us from irresponsible inertia. Give us not over to any death of the soul, but lift us into newness of life, that we may use this day of opportunity and danger to serve Thee, yea, to glorify Thee and enjoy Thee forever; in the Spirit of Thy Son whose voice wakes the dead and whose Word giveth life. Amen.*

5

Mankind's Unfailing Lamp

Thy Word is a lamp unto my feet, and a light unto my path.   PSALM 119:105

ONE late afternoon I called at an apartment on the sixth floor of one of our modern apartment buildings. As I turned to leave, the lights went out due to a "power cut-off." The good lady who escorted me to the door handed me an electric flashlight. "Take this, otherwise you won't be able to see your way down the stairs and through the corridors. Leave it with the doorman as you go out." She was right. I needed that light. It was not a powerful searchlight; it did not illumine the entire building nor did I need any such powerful illumination. Gratefully, I shone it at my feet and walked safely down the stairs and through the blacked-out building.

Psalm 119 speaks of the Bible in terms of such a light. "Thy Word is a lamp unto my feet, and a light unto my path." We need that light. Bertrand Russell once said that "the life of man is a long march through the night." But we who stand in the Hebrew-Christian tradition have something more to say than that. From the Old Testament and more especially from the New Testament the divine Voice calls to our hearts, Never fear! Travel on. No night is so dark but God will see that there is a light in our darkness. The glory of our Faith is that no one need miss his way; God provides light in the dark to walk by. There is the illumination furnished by the Holy Spirit. He is the light that lighteth every man that comes into the world, and journeys through it. He is the inner Light. The light shines in the darkness to give the light of the glory of the knowledge of God in the

46

person of Jesus Christ. But we should never have known of that light without the unfailing lamp of the Bible.

The Psalmist does not claim too much for this lamp. Nowhere does he or any of the other writers of Scripture say that the lamp does not carry the flaws of its human makers. He does not claim that the book is a textbook of science, nor a blueprint of present-day world events, "a kind of knotty puzzle, to which if you are clever enough, you can find the key and so peer into the future." Young people who discover the human factors which operated in its composition and translation are apt to conclude that it is merely ancient literature, a museum of literary antiquities, quaint legends, primitive interpretations, outmoded concepts. But misinformed individuals need to be reminded that "mercifully, we need not be a scientist to be men of God"; that "God could and did speak to men who believed this earth was flat, just as today He speaks to shepherds on the hillside and sailors on the high seas who could by no means comprehend the marvels of God's universe which Einstein has discovered."[1]

Let us be careful to claim for the Bible what it claims for itself: "Thy Word is a lamp unto my feet, and a light unto my path," not a blazing searchlight uncovering all the mysteries of the universe and human history, but a light sufficient to make the next step clear and keep the wayfarer from falling.

You see the picture: a man trudging through the dark, picking his way through unknown country by the light of a lantern. His lantern does not light up the whole scene, but it makes the immediate path clear so that he can walk warily and well the road he must take. So this Book does not give light upon every conceivable matter, but it does light our way, show us our duty, reveal the divine Guide and Companion, and make clear the Road Home. In simple words, the Bible is supremely a religious book, the religious book. Within its sixty-six books we discern its own progressive character. The early parts reflect the infancy of the race. Think of how its light upon the character of God increases, from kindergarten pictures to Amos with his mature conception of God as moral judge, Isaiah discovering His Holiness, Hosea finding God as infinite Mercy, until the full illumination floods the mind in Jesus, the Light of the World, revealing God in all His holy, righteous, fatherly and redemptive Love. The old leads up to the new, the new finds its beginnings in the old. Never does the Bible falter in its witness to God. Even though men as different in language and style as Bunyan and the present Archbishop of Canterbury, or Chaucer and Lloyd Douglas, are among its writers, doing their work in thirteen different centuries, there is an astonishing and wonderful unity about this library. It is unity like that of a symphony or of a drama moving steadily toward its climax. "It is acknowledged as the Word of God because through it generation after generation, God speaks to men's souls."

I

"Thy Word is a lamp unto my feet, and a light unto my path."

Consider with me how this Lamp gives unfailing light. We might speak of it as a three-purpose lamp.[2]

For one thing, it is *the book of the beautiful*. Not only because as Keats said, "Truth is beauty," but because of its incomparable poetry and prose, its haunting expression of timeless insights and events, is this Lamp itself beautiful and in turn the means whereby we perceive the beautiful. Renan, the French critic and man of letters, described the Gospel according to St. Luke as "the most beautiful book ever written." It is not extravagant to extend that title to the Bible as a whole. The most familiar version, the authorized King James Version, has been called "the noblest monument of English prose." Modern translations are extremely helpful in understanding obscure passages, but for sheer beauty of diction nothing has surpassed the older English version. Recently, Professor E. J. Pratt, distinguished Canadian poet and teacher of literature, reviewed an anthology of religious poetry. In his review he confessed that he looked first of all to see whether the compiler had included within his mas-

terpieces of religious poetry the superb epic poem in the Book of
Job, "The Voice out of the Whirlwind." When he found it, he
decided that this anthologist had good standards of selection and
was acquainted with the best. You remember how it begins:

> Where wast thou when I laid the foundations of the earth?
> . . . When the morning stars sang together,
> And all the sons of God shouted for joy?

You will have other favorite passages. How skillfully the transla-
tors chose their words from our rich vocabulary! They preferred,
for the most part, short words: "Blessed are the pure in heart,
for they shall see God." In Ruth, how the wording matches the
setting: "The Lord do so to me, and more also, if aught but death
part me and thee." (Seventeen words and only eighteen syllables!)
They knew, too, how to employ "sonorous Latinisms": "Now
unto the King eternal, immortal, invisible. . . ." "This corruption shall put on incorruption, and this mortal shall put on
immortality. . . ." Say aloud to catch the stately rhythm of the
opening words: "In the beginning God created the heaven and
the earth. And the earth was without form, and void; and darkness was upon the face of the deep. And the Spirit of God moved
upon the face of the waters. And God said, let there be light:
and there was light." Or the impassioned cry of the prophet
Amos: "The lion hath roared, who will not fear? The Lord God
hath spoken, who can but prophesy?" Or the singing beauty of
Isaiah: "How beautiful upon the mountains are the feet of him
that bringeth good tidings, that publisheth peace; that bringeth
good tidings of good, that publisheth salvation; that saith unto
Zion, Thy God reigneth!" Mark the superb economy of words in
this: "The soul of Jonathan was knit with the soul of David, and
Jonathan loved him as his own soul." The more lyrical beauty of
the Psalms: "The Lord is my shepherd, I shall not want." "The
Lord is my light and my salvation; whom shall I fear? The Lord
is the strength of my life; of whom shall I be afraid?"

Turning to the New Testament, who would deprive himself of

the idyllic loveliness of the story of the birth of Christ? The
parables are significant, of course, for what they say, but also for
the "luminous simplicity with which they say it." Read with a
discerning eye that unsurpassed short story told by the Master
which begins, "A certain man had two sons . . ." As for the apostle Paul's writing, his great expression of great thoughts loses
nothing in English translation: "Though I speak with the
tongues of men and of angels, and have not charity, I am become
as sounding brass, or a tinkling cymbal." Elsewhere one comes
upon sentences "that in sudden gleaming beauty shine like
stars": "Let the peace of God rule in yours hearts." "Be strong in
the Lord, and in the power of his might." "He looked for a city
which hath foundations, whose builder and maker is God." "They
need no candle, neither light of the sun; for the Lord God giveth
them light."

II

"Thy word is a lamp unto my feet, *and a light unto my path.*"
This unfailing lamp shines on the road we travel. Consider the
Bible as a guidebook. In the New Testament Christianity is
described as "The Way," Christians as "men and women . . . who
belonged to the Way."[3] In the Old Testament there are frequent
references to the religious life as walking the way or the path.
The metaphor is a good one. Life is a pilgrimage, a journey, and
we need a road map. The Bible provides it. It indicates the route,
marks the road, points out the highway to God. If you have done
much motoring, you must be grateful for makers of maps and
for the unknown benefactors of travelers who erected road signs
and route markers. "Similarly," writes Dean Corwin C. Roach,[4]
"the way of God has been charted, mapped and marked by countless millions of men who have lived and died, most of them
nameless. They have posted the road, at first but a part of the
road, for the mountain peak of death loomed up too loft, too
forbidding for them to surmount, until there came One, Who
calling Himself the Way, marked the highway from start to fin-

ish." Great indeed was the company who labored to record the Word of God, to preserve it, and to transmit it. How different they were, and yet how one they were in their conviction that life is from God, in God, and to God. So we may speak of the Book they gave us as "an age-long diary recording the search of man for an understanding of God," and also as the record of God's age-long search for man. It is indeed a guide for our lives. To those who seek its wisdom and follow its truth, it is indeed an unfailing lamp casting its beams down through the days and years. Modern wayfarers seek its guidance. Someone inquired at a great reference library and learned that the Bible is often called for. (In spite of the magnificent work of our Bible societies in distributing the Scriptures, evidently many North Americans lack copies of their own.) Moreover, all of the many copies available are thumb-scarred at identical spots—the Christmas story in Luke, the Sermon on the Mount in Matthew, the Psalms, the poetry of Job, the fourteenth of John, and other passages that speak to the varied needs of pilgrims. The Bible begins in a garden and ends in the City of God. Through the most exalted pages of the Old Testament, and in the New with vivid clarity, the way is marked. The vision of man's pilgrimage to the goal purposed by the Eternal God shines: "I am the way, the truth and the life. . . ."[5] "And I, John, saw the holy city, new Jerusalem, coming down from God out of heaven, prepared as a bride adorned for her husband."[6] "And the ransomed of the Lord shall return, and come to Zion with songs and everlasting joy upon their heads; they shall obtain joy and gladness, and sorrow and sighing shall flee away."[7]

The Psalmist spoke of God's Word as light—"a light unto my path." Light is one of the great words of the Scriptures, and so is Life. And both are closely related. Scientists have made fascinating discoveries concerning light and have shown us how the simple ray of sunlight takes to itself the wonder and mystery of the divine. We know of particular rays which stimulate our health and the growth of vegetation. On the other hand, other

rays of light are successfully used to destroy disease-producing
germs, bacteria. The photo-electric cell has many beneficent uses,
and its basic principle is a beam of light. So the Bible is a many-
colored light which releases power within the mind and soul of
the person who reads it reverently, intelligently, expectantly.
Light has always been associated with life. How early and how
widespread has been man's worship of the sun as the source of
life! In many Psalms God is spoken of as the Sun, whose beams
carry healing. Drugstores advertise products which are called
"bottled sunshine." We might apply that phrase to the Bible. As
nowhere else, we find within this Book concentrated life-giving
power.

Who does not need power? You and I need power to live decently and well, power to manage human relationships, power to
do one's duty however irksome, power to overcome temptation
and to replace bad habits with wholesome ones, power to run a
straight race, to keep on doggedly when the terrain is difficult
and the energy flags; power to handle well adversity and pros-
perity, power to triumph over disaster and sorrow, moral failure
and death. Here is power. When a British monarch is crowned,
the Archbishop of Canterbury takes a volume and places it in
the new king's or queen's hands. "We present you with this book,"
he says, "the most valuable thing that this world affords. Here is
wisdom, this is the Royal Law; these are the lively oracles of
God." That volume, of course, is a copy of the Bible. King and
queen and commoner alike have this source of personal power.
The reason why so many of us are spiritually anemic is that our
spiritual diet has been poor, deficient in life-giving vitamins.
The central figure of the New Testament, the Word of God
incarnate, declares: "The words I speak unto you they are spirit
and they are *life*." I read of a woman who gave her physician a
long list of her symptoms and answered his questions. She was
astonished at his prescription. "Madam, what you need is to read
your Bible more. Go home and read it an hour a day and then
come back to me a month from today." In a month she returned

to his office. "Well," he said, "I see you are an obedient patient and have taken my prescription faithfully. Do you feel as if you needed any other medicine?" "No, doctor," she said, "I don't. I feel like a different person. But how did you know that was just what I needed?" Power for healing us of our self-despisings, for curing us of our basic fears, power for useful, outgoing living is often transmitted to us by the Spirit of God through the Book of books. Too many in every age have found it there for us to be skeptical or indifferent. For within its pages we encounter the source of all power and wisdom and love, the God who has said through His Son Jesus, "All power is given unto me . . . go ye. . . ."

But the power made available through the Bible is not alone for our solitariness. It speaks to us together, in community; to the nation, to the nations. It sets moral standards. It insists on recognition of the dignity of man, of his rights as a child of God made in His image. It sets forth justice as the will of God, and human unity in brotherhood and peace as the purpose of God. It reveals the righteous will of God active in history, and as sovereign over history—a righteous will to which finally all men and all nations are accountable. It is through the revealing Word of this Book that we encounter the Power that makes for righteousness, the Power which enables frail children of earth to work miracles of social transformation. Said Sir Wilfred Grenfell, "I am absolutely sure that familiarity with the Bible adds a permanent power to man's life. It is the one and only book holding out any hope for the realization of a permanent world peace." And H. G. Wells surprisingly asserted that "the Bible is the book that has held together the fabric of Western civilization. . . . We want a Bible," he added, "so badly that we cannot afford to put the old Bible on a pinnacle out of daily use."

That is the conclusion of the matter. Take the Book off its pinnacle. When the blackout descends, you have a lamp. Use it. Before the darkness falls, become familiar with this unfailing light. Before you journey far, become bewildered or lost, study this road map. When you need strength for daily living, and before you are conscious of such need, make regular devotional reading of the Book of books part of your spiritual diet.

How shall you read it so that it may be pleasant as well as profitable? Here are a few suggestions:

1. Obtain a Bible which appeals to you both in its type and format.

2. Secure a few supplemental helps: a modern translation such as Moffatt's, Goodspeed's, Weymouth's, or the recent Revised Standard Version; a one-volume Bible dictionary and a brief concordance.

3. Set aside a regular time each day to read it. One man tries to retire fifteen minutes earlier each night in order to have an extra fifteen minutes each morning for reading.

4. Follow a scheme of Bible readings such as may be found in devotional books, magazines such as *The Upper Room,* or the leaflets of the Bible Reading Fellowship.

5. Read the Bible books as you would others, not in snippets or unrelated passages. Who would think of reading a short story in four sittings? The Book of Ruth is a short story and can be read in twenty minutes. Did you know that half of the shorter books of our Scriptures can each be read in less than forty-five minutes?

6. Finally, read with imagination, intellect and will engaged. Get the picture; imagine yourself present. Put your mind on it so that you gain some idea of what the writer intended, and what God may intend it to mean to you today. (What notion or what practice of mine does this challenge?) Then, let it engage your will: what must be done because of this? How may I relate the truth to my life? Is there anything I ought to do this day in the light of it?

Thus you will realize in your own experience that God has given you in the Scriptures an unfailing lamp. With confidence and in deep serenity and joy you will walk in that Light till traveling days are done.

PRAYER: *May we hide Thy words in our hearts, O God, think upon them with our minds, obey them with our lives, and proclaim them with our lips. So may Thy salvation come even unto us, according to Thy Word, and in every dark and difficult way may Thy Word be a lantern to our feet and a light upon our path; we ask it in the name of Him who is Thy Word made manifest, our Saviour Jesus Christ. Amen.*

6

Christmas Unlimited

And the Word became flesh, and dwelt among us.   JOHN 1:14 (R.S.V.)

The Word became flesh, and lived awhile in our midst.   (Weymouth)

The Word became flesh and blood and lived for a while among us.
(Goodspeed)

That Christ may dwell in your hearts through faith.   EPHESIANS 3:17 (R.S.V.)

I pray that Christ may make His home in your hearts through your faith.
(Weymouth)

H AVE you ever felt that a regrettable feature of Christmas is
that there is so little of it? So much anticipation, so many
preparations, then so limited a time of celebration. Of course, in
one sense we are grateful that Christmas comes but once a year.
Pity the poor parents with their depleted energies and exchequers
if it came oftener! Consider the plight of salespeople in our
crowded stores if Christmas were prolonged indefinitely. Yes,
obviously, there is a sense in which the Festival must be limited
in duration. For a more spiritual reason the Feast cannot be continued day after day. The Christmas season is a mountaintop in
the landscape of the year; we climb with willing feet, however
weary, and find on its heights exhilarating air, enkindling vision,
and rediscover a Way, a Message, and a Light. Yet we cannot live
day after day on the most glorious mountain peak. Permanent
residence on a lofty summit would make us neglect the duties in
the valleys. It is on the plains that the necessary if humdrum
tasks of life for the most part are done.

But why should we limit "Operation Christmas" to one brief
period, to one blessed Day? that is the question.

One evening toward the end of January a householder was

astonished to hear a child's voice singing "Hark! the herald angels sing" at his front door. He went to investigate the anachronism. "Don't you know that Christmas was a month ago?" he asked. "Yes sir," said the pale little singer, "but I had measles then and couldn't go out caroling." Is it equally absurd for men and women to try to keep the angelic song echoing when Christmas is over and gone? For a few days prior to the anniversary we let the spirit of Christmas have its gentle, relaxing way with us. To use words written by Henry van Dyke:

> [We] are willing to forget what we have done for other people, and to remember what other people have done for us; to ignore what the world owes us, and think what we owe the world; to put our rights in the background, our duties in the middle distance, and our chances to do a little more than our duty in the foreground—to own that probably the only good reason for our existence is not what we are going to get out of life, but what we are going to give life . . . to trim our lamp so that it will give more light and less smoke, and carry it in front so that our shadow will fall behind us; to make a grave for our ugly thoughts and a garden for our kindly feelings, with the gate open.

We are willing to do these things for a day or two, and thus we keep Christmas. If we are Christians we do more: we are willing to believe that "the blessed life which began in Bethlehem more than nineteen hundred years ago is the image and brightness of Eternal Love." That is really keeping Christmas.

Why not always?

> Gone is the rustle of the wings,
> Heard in the watch serene;
> The Golden Hour of God is past . . .

Why should it be gone and past for us? Perhaps it is because we accept the historic fact without accepting its present power. It could be because we have kept Christmas in our homes and offices, in our clubs and churches, at our parties and festivals, and not in our hearts. Does that sound ridiculously simple and hopelessly antiquated?

If you turn to the New Testament you will see that the fact which Christmas commemorates has both limited and unlimited significance. You might say that one verse presents Christ's birth historically, the other verse setting forth the reality of Christ's coming mystically. One without the other is inadequate, a partial truth. The first verse is from the prologue to John's Gospel: verse fourteen of the first chapter: "The Word became flesh and dwelt among us." The second verse is from the Epistle to the Ephesians, chapter three, verse seventeen: "That Christ may dwell in your hearts by faith." In these two verses past and present are linked so that the reality in its total meaning is set before us. It is interesting to note that two different words are used. In John's sentence, the verb suggests a brief visit: "He *tented* amongst us." Weymouth's modern translation renders it: "The Word became flesh and lived a while in our midst." Dr. Goodspeed translates it similarly, "The Word became flesh and blood and lived for a while among us." Dr. Moffatt's word is "tarried."

In the apostle's statement the word used is like our word "house"; Paul prays that God will enable Christ "to house himself in our hearts." Weymouth gives this vivid translation: "I pray that Christ may make His home in your hearts through your faith."

You and I need this blending of historic fact and personal experience if we would keep Christmas throughout the years of our lives. A British preacher of acute mind, Frederick C. Spurr, phrased it clearly: "A Christ only historic is no more value than Socrates or Plato. A Christ only mystical is of half value, being severed from the historic source."

Here then is *Christmas limited,* that which a thinker of the schools might call the transient Incarnation: "The Word became flesh and lived for a while among us." The entrance of God into human life in the most vital fashion was a "tenting" amongst men. St. John could turn to the Greek thinkers, using their own word "logos," the divine Reason, the Mind of the Universe, and could say, "Your logos, we have seen Him; your hypothetical and impalpable Being we have handled. . . . He is substantial—He has worn our robe of flesh and blood. He has lived among us."[1]

He is God's Word to us. "Word"—a word may conceal thought; it may also reveal character and spirit. One has said, "As your words express you, and vocalize your thought, so Christ utters God. In Him we see and hear God." The Divine is in league with us. Without God, man is but a fitful spark of life flickering briefly in an indifferent universe, the sport of fate to be snuffed out at death. But measured by the fact of the incarnation, man is kin to the Eternal, a child of the divine Father. This means that man is the object of God's love and care; that in His sight you and I are worth saving. It means that we can be liberated from our animal inheritance into the freedom of the sons and daughters of God. We can be lifted into beauty, into truth, and into love, and in our best hours it is this transformation that we desire more than anything else.

The twenty-nine years of the earthly life of Jesus is a demonstration in visible human personality of that which we seek. In the total event of His life—His teaching, His mighty acts, His death and resurrection, His continued life within His Body the Church—He shows God the Father, and God as Saviour and Friend. He proves man capable of redemption. Therefore we may not measure the value of the historic incarnation. God's action and disclosure in Jesus Christ has impressed human life indelibly.

> God may have other words for other worlds,
> But the Word of God for this world is Christ.

Nevertheless, there is a sense in which the limited Christmas fact makes us feel as if we had been defrauded. Others knew Him; but His generation alone seems to have experienced the firsthand vital benefits. He seems so remote from us. More than one lover of His spirit has sighed wistfully, "I would like to have been with Him then." To overcome this limitation of the transient incarnation men have sought to live with Him by imagination. John Ruskin wisely urged this method of reading the Gospel story. Try to imagine yourself present when He healed this sufferer, when He interviewed this inquirer, advised Ruskin. Others have reduced the remoteness of the historic Jesus by trying to fix Him in the Sacrament, making Him for high devotional purposes the "Prisoner of the Altar." But such worship however sincere and pious provides no genuine transcending of the past, for one practice limits him to the past, and the other to a place and to a priest. So we come to the truth of *Christmas unlimited*: to the inwardness of the incarnation whereby the Lord Christ becomes a present, ennobling reality. "I pray," writes Paul, "I pray that Christ may make His home in your hearts through your faith." The incarnation must be continuous if it is to benefit us, and through us creatively to affect our contemporaries. Manifestly, this is impossible in the "tenting" form. His permanent incarnation is spiritual, "in your heart." Is not the only way in which a person can really dwell with us through residence "in our hearts"?

A person may live in the same house with us, in the same apartment, and yet emotionally and spiritually live miles removed from us. Conversely, a person may live thousands of miles distant from us, so that we never see him or hear him or speak to him, for months, even years, and yet live with us. Absence makes the heart grow fonder of someone else, says the cynic. To which the voice of our own experience answers: not when the absent one is loved and loving! Love is deepened, love is strengthened when one who has "tented" beside us has gone away. Have you never had the sense of a presence of someone who wandered away into the Unseen? Have you not, without being the least bit "psychic," felt the loved one near?

So is it with Christ, only in a manner more profound than with any human friend. By the power of the divine Spirit, He "indwells" us, not physically, not poetically, and more than sacramentally. He is a real spiritual presence living within us. There is a real bond between us and Him and an ever-deepening communion words are impotent to describe. He can mold us as we let

Him dominate us by His Spirit. This Spirit is more than a fancy or nebulous influence; it is a force communicated directly to us. "That Christ may be housed in your hearts by faith." Such faith is not a vague intellectual belief; it is a tuning in to the vibrations proceeding from a real presence in the spiritual realm. Christ does live in men and women. Not in all men for some will not receive Him. But He still waits at the threshold of every personality: "Behold I stand at the door. . . ." He still offers: "The water that I shall give him shall become in him a well of water, springing up into eternal life." He still promises: "If any man thirst, let him come unto Me and drink. He that believeth on Me . . . shall know." "This spake He of the Spirit which they that believe on Him were to receive."[2] All these figures of speech point to the primary truth that all who open their lives to Him find a new life developing, the very quality of life which He lived in all of its fullness. Only this reproducible experience makes sense of such New Testament affirmations as, "Christ in you, the hope of glory," "Christ liveth in me." Here is no new mysticism, but the testimony of valid spiritual experience through the ages. The Master Himself found it hard to convince His own disciples that He could go away from them and yet be with them "all the days." Yet this is what He affirmed repeatedly; and He identified Himself with the Spirit of God. "I will not leave you desolate: I will come to you."[3] We will come unto Him and make our home [abode] with Him. According to St. John His last prayer for His disciples contained the sublime petition: "that the love with which thou hast loved Me may be in them *and I in them*."[4]

So down through the centuries men and women, even as you and I, have been aware of being controlled and molded by a dynamic Presence. You may recall Tolstoy's tribute to Lincoln on hearing of the great emancipator's death: "He was a Christ in miniature." That is what we are to become—Christs in miniature. Has it ever been done? Let Christian biography submit the evidence. A few illustrious examples come quickly to mind. Francis of Assisi in the twelfth century reincarnated Christ. John

Bunyan's tale of the Pilgrim moved Gladstone to exclaim: "No tinker hath such powers as this. It is my belief that in Bunyan God spoke." George Whitefield said of Isaac Watts, "He was a bit of Christ." Once two ruffians decided to stop Wesley's evangelistic mission by injuring the evangelist. They reached their arms back, each hand clutching stones. Wesley spoke of the power of Christ to change life, and as he spoke such a beauty spread over his face that the two misguided men stood transfixed. One turned to the other and said, "He ain't a man, Bill. He ain't a man." The stones rolled from their hands to the ground. As Wesley continued speaking—offering them Christ as he described it—their hearts were softened. When the service had ended, and Wesley made his way through the crowd, the listeners stood aside respectfully to let him pass. One of the ruffians put out his hand to touch the hem of the preacher's garment, and as he did so Wesley's attention was drawn to him and his companion. He reached out his two hands, placed them on their heads and said, "God bless you, my boys," and passed on. As he left, one man said to the other, with even more awe in his voice: "He is a man, Bill. He is a man. He's a man like God." Again and again, in less dramatic fashion than in the episode from Wesley's life, men and women have released the transforming power of Christ because Christ had made His home in their souls through their commitment to Him in trust and obedience.

How will you reproduce this miracle of Christmas unlimited? You can begin by turning to that life as it shines through the Gospels. As God in Christ confronts you in your need and longing, you respond with such faith as He Himself will supply. Then submit to the gentle imperiousness of the living Lord. His dealings with you will be those of the divine contemporary. Said Sir Wilfred Grenfell: "Faith came to me with the vision of Christ still alive in this world today. He meant to me a determination, God helping me, to follow Him." In prayer and meditation, in worship together with other seekers within the fellowship of His Church, let your imagination bring Him near. As He grows more real and more commanding, you will find ways in which you can express Him and His will to your generation and within your community. Almost before you know it you will have high company, even the warm, comforting and quickening companionship of the living Lord. Down a secret stair of His own contriving, He will come to the inn of your inner life. Happy are you if you make room for Him there!

PRAYER: *O God, who makest us glad with the yearly remembrance of the birth of Thy Son Jesus Christ, grant us Thy grace that we may know Him daily as our Redeemer, Companion and Guide who ever liveth and reigneth with Thee and the Holy Spirit, one God, world without end. Amen.*

A CHRISTMAS BENEDICTION: *May the power of the Most High, the lowliness of Jesus Christ, and the overshadowing of the Holy Spirit give you peace, and love, and everlasting joy. Amen.*

7
Where Did Christmas Go?

And the shepherds returned, glorifying and praising God for all the things they had heard and seen.   LUKE 2:20

And being warned of God in a dream . . . they departed into their own country another way.   MATTHEW 2:12

And the child grew, and waxed strong in spirit, filled with wisdom: and the grace of God was upon Him.   LUKE 2:40

WHEN we were very young it caused real perplexity: where did Christmas go? Weeks of preparation, anticipation, even some recreation—then the swift hours of realization—and for parents something like prostration. And Christmas had gone. Back to commonplace days and tasks; and the Christmas tree looking more tired every day, and the tinsel tarnishing. Grownups feel the abrupt shift of interest and emphasis, too. For all too short a time everybody seems to be enjoying a huge love affair which chases away all the wrinkles of the year. Human beings are at their best; if you hold a hopeful view of human nature you will say, human nature is itself—generous, friendly, kind. Then back to earth from the starlight—with a thud. Where does Christmas go?

One modern poet, George Edward Hoffman, felt its disappearance somewhat sharply. He wrote eight lines and called them "December 26":

> Chants, incense, and the glory pass and die:
>   The festive lights diminish; solemn prayer
> Gives way to ribald song and pageantry,
>   And market cries again confuse the square.

64

> And He whose spirit held us for one day,
> Seeing love consumed again by doubt and fear,
> Sorrowing, returns the long and thorny way
> Until we make Him welcome through the year.[1]

The authors of our source material for the Christmas Story—Matthew and Luke—gave us clues as to where the original Christmas actors went. Neither Gospel writer tells us much, but enough for thought and imagination to work on.

Where did the Bethlehem shepherds go? "The shepherds returned, glorifying and praising God for all the things they had heard and seen," says Luke. Returned where? Why, returned to their business of sheep-tending! "Life is so daily" for most of us. It was so for those shepherds. A supernal revelation had been granted them. A sky-born music would echo through their souls to the very end of their lives. But meanwhile, there were the sheep to be tended, pastures to be cultivated, fences to be mended—and the lambs to be helped into the world and guarded. There was wool to be sheared, and sold, and the other workaday jobs to be done.

Life is like that for most of us. In the very nature of things it cannot be one long holiday, nor would any ideal design for living make it so. Of course, in spite of five-day weeks becoming the accepted arrangement, and increasing holidays, many of the world's workers still toil too long hours, at monotonous work, with little leisure for creative activity of their own choosing.

But, thinking again of the shepherds—and of us, too—is the question not this: not, Where did they go?—but How?

> It is not so much *where* you live,
> As *how*, and *why*, and *when* you live,
> That answers in the affirmative,
> Or maybe in the negative,
> ....
> The question—Are you fit to live?
> It is not so much *where* you live,
> As whether while you live you *live*

And to the world your highest give,
And so make answer positive
That you are truly fit to live.[2]

The Bethlehem shepherds returned to their jobs; that is commonplace. But they returned "glorifying and praising God for all the things they had heard and seen." That is distinctly uncommon; and requires religion to account for it. They "returned glorifying God": what does that mean for persons like ourselves—who must go back to the old office, or shop, or kitchen sink, or woodpile, or whatever!—now that Christmas has gone for another year? Surely it is that because of the profound meaning of Christmas—that God has visited and redeemed His people through a human personality, that the Eternal is forever breaking through in time in Christlike power and beauty—we shall have what Schweitzer of Africa would call a new "reverence for life." And new interest in its possibilities. You remember reading of the fine Negro engineer on a Southern river boat who was asked by Archibald Rutledge how he kept everything in such perfect working order and so immaculately clean. As he laid down a Bible he had been reading quietly, the engineer explained: "I've got a glory." You and I must have a glory, if we are to do more than get up, wash our faces, work, and go to bed—day after day. To see life as given us by a wonderful God; to know that life is invested with deathless meaning and invincible dignity; to be transmitters of His loving-kindness—because God came in Jesus Christ—is to have a glory.

To be glad for life, and the march of days; to be grateful for one's comrades, generous, loyal and kind; to be immensely pleased that there are opportunities to do some helpful things, without any thought or wish for recognition; to be able to pray and know that whether hopes come through or not, the prayer is heard, and the pray-er answered; to do one's part to make the living Church of God what God intends it to be—the serviceable fellowship of the spirit of Christ: surely this is part of returning to our particular fields after Christmas—"glorifying and praising God."

There is an old spiritual, which Tin Pan Alley may have borrowed without so much as "by your leave," which has a recurring refrain: "Rise, shine, give God the glory!" That is it. Paul meant precisely that when he said: "Whether therefore ye eat, or drink, or whatsoever ye do, do all to the glory of God."[3] The commonplace details of daily life can be—are to be—lifted up as participants in the splendid enterprise God inaugurated—and glorified.

Where did Christmas go? It depends on you—you and God! The shepherds would never be the same, nor their work. Don't you think each one of them went back saying to himself, "I keep sheep for God"? Jenny Lind, the Swedish nightingale, summed up the difference Christ had made when she said, "I sing for God." Christmas continues when a person says, "I do business for God . . ." "I teach school for God . . ." "I farm—for God . . ." "I drive a truck, a taxi, a plane, a train—for God . . ." "I nurse for God . . ." "I practice medicine for God . . ." Isn't that keeping the Christmas radiance all through the year? Don't you think glory will shine through luminous, active persons of that spirit?

Where did the wise men go? Here again we have the terse detail given by Matthew: "Being warned of God in a dream . . . they departed into their own country another way." Of course it means that they outwitted Herod by taking a different route home than the one they used to come on their eventful journey. Here again, the important question is not WHERE, but HOW they went back from Christmas. I am sure—aren't you?—that they returned *wiser* men; wiser because they had followed a gleam—a clue; wiser because they had really looked into the face of a newborn child and seen the reality and loveliness and potential of the God who creates planets and universes! They knew, as a Hebrew poet knew, that the Vast Wisdom that "tellest the number of the stars" also "healeth the broken in heart." They saw not in a glorious star, but in a Holy Family, the disclosure of divine reality they sought. They returned wiser men because in Christ they had found the Infinite drawing near; and had knelt in adoration before the Holy Child. They had found God in the most unlikely place—out back in a stable! Now they would be on the alert for signs of His presence everywhere.

They returned happier because they returned "lighter"! They had come bringing gifts. They returned without their gifts but with that indescribable lightness of heart which every generous giver knows. They had left their burden of gold, incense and perfume with the Holy Family. Life would be easier for those Displaced Persons now that they had money with which to pay their way in Egypt, and carried fragrant tokens of God's watchful care. How easy it is to dismiss all the Christmas giving as silly, sentimental and extravagant! But not all of it can be so dismissed or condemned. Some of it, doubtless, deserves criticism. But when we give for Love's sake, to ease the burden for some other hard-bestead pilgrim—to say "Thank you!" for uncommon thoughtfulness, for devotion beyond the requirements of duty, to make another's New Year new in hope and perhaps in health—such giving makes not only the pocketbook lighter—but the heart, too.

The wise men returned wiser, and happier; confident now, with their chief questions answered. Are we returning from Christmas that way? If so, Christmas will not vanish; not its essential spirit, its grace, its glory. A child heard her mother read aloud the famous Gospel within the Gospel of St. John: "For God so loved that He gave His only begotten Son." Said the mother, "Isn't that wonderful?" "I don't think so," said the child honestly. "It would be for anyone else, but not God. It is like Him to give . . ."

One more query concerning the chief participants in the first Christmas? *Where did the central Figure go?* One tells of a child, hearing her mother read the Christmas narrative out of a child's Bible storybook. She asked her mother after she had read about the wise men returning to their own country: "Mother, did the Baby Jesus live happily ever afterward?" To the child's mind the beautiful story appealed as a fairy story would. And a child expects a happy ending at the close of a lovely fairy tale. Well, we are dealing with no fairy story, or legend, when we encounter the Fact of Christ. Let no one imagine that the drama which began at Bethlehem ended there or that one can write concerning the Holy Family: "And they lived happily ever afterward." Taken by itself the Christmas story seems idyllic, so "out-of-this-world" in its ethereal beauty. Angels and kings and strong shepherds coming and going from the wings of the stage. But the total story is as real as a brutal dictator; as real as refugees trying to escape destruction; as real as hatred. "The angel of the Lord appeareth to Joseph in a dream, saying, Arise and take the young child and his mother, and flee into Egypt, and be thou there until I bring thee word: for Herod will seek the young child to destroy him."[4] Usually a Nativity play ends with the groups around the manger, and the various visitors, human and celestial, making inconspicuous exits down the aisles. But the Greatest Drama in the world does not end that way. There is the Flight into Egypt, the return to Nazareth, the long years of toil and preparation in carpenter shop and home, the helping of the widowed mother and dependent family; then the brief public ministry of healing and teaching; the inevitable clash with the powers of darkness; the conflict with practical atheism (some of it wearing ecclesiastical robes) ; the arrest, the trial and the execution.

Where did the Baby Jesus go? Luke set it down: "And the child grew and waxed strong in spirit, filled with wisdom: and the grace of God was upon Him."[5] But that grace conferred no immunity from the slings and arrows of outrageous malevolence and stupidity, nor from the sting of pain, the ache of exhaustion. Where do babies generally go? Into childhood, adolescence, adulthood . . . Do you know Eleanor Slater's lines which she calls "December Twenty-fourth"?

> Tomorrow You are born again
> Who died so many times.
> Do You like the candle-light,
> Do You like the chimes?

Do You stop to wonder
Why men never see
How very closely Bethlehem
Approaches Calvary?[6]

Why did the Babe of Bethlehem become the Christ of Calvary?
The truest answer I know is that of the New Testament: God
"made Himself of no reputation and took upon Him the form of
a servant, and was made in the likeness of men. He humbled
Himself and became obedient unto death, even the death of the
Cross."[7]

Where did Christmas go? Too often it goes into the attic, the
storeroom, the file marked "Next Year." But the Christ who
makes Christmas went on, through life, and death, and through
death that you and I might have life and healing, forgiveness,
hope, and everlasting joy. So today, even if mysticism mystifies and
annoys you, you can say with a man of insight who wrote over
three hundred years ago:

He is a path, if any be misled;
   He is a robe, if any naked be;
If any chance to hunger, he is bread;
   If any be a bondman, he is free;
   If any be but weak, how strong is he!
To dead men life he is, to sick men health;
To blind men, sight, and to the needy, wealth;
A pleasure without loss, a treasure without stealth.[8]

Christ has not gone from our world. Said the centurion to Procula
after the crucifixion,[9] "He is let loose in the world, lady, where
neither Roman nor Jew can stop His truth." In spite of all that
discourages, He has been making us more sensitive to human
need, more concerned about justice and mercy. He is a catalytic
force, working quietly and steadily in our hearts and in the heart
of mankind.

There is a question before the house—your house, my house.
It is this: Where are *you* going from Bethlehem? Do you know

where you are going? And whom you will follow, and *Who* is going with you?

PRAYER: *O God and Father of us all, who hast given us thyself supremely in Christ: we give thee thanks that He has walked the second mile from Bethlehem, that Thy love incarnate in Christ still keeps comradeship with men. May we who so often think ourselves wise, grow simple in trust and insight, and discover where He is, and follow where He leads. Amen.*

8

A Condition Men Forget

Ye shall not see my face, except your brother be with you.   GENESIS 43:5

LIKE many of the great plays of Shakespeare, the story of Joseph and his brethren is a drama of reconciliation. When the brothers grovel before the Prince whose true identity is unknown to them, the requirements of rough justice are met. The man who was cruelly wronged now stands in the place of power. Joseph, thrown into a pit twenty years earlier by these same men, is now able to hurl them into the depths of despair from which only he may rescue them. Happily, magnanimity and fraternal affection triumphed over any passion for revenge in Joseph's soul. He would help them, but on one condition. Before their petition for aid could be granted, this instruction was to be carried out to the letter: they were to return to the old home, and bring back to him their youngest brother as hostage. Only so could they escape the ravages of famine riding relentlessly over the land. The chastened delegation went home. The food they brought was only sufficient to tide them over a few days. Return to Egypt for a more adequate supply, they informed their father, was only possible on one condition, namely, that his beloved Benjamin go with them and remain in the custody of the Egyptian prime minister. To the old father's heartbroken protests they repeated the inexorable word spoken to them: "Ye shall not see my face, except your brother be with you." Painful memories were stirred by that command. Their old crime haunted them more vividly than ever. The Prince had spoken of Benjamin; their minds raced back to another brother believed lost beyond recall. But there it was.

72

Starvation, perhaps unto death, was the grim alternative. "Ye shall not see my face, except your brother be with you."

To the perceptive Christian, the ancient tale flashes meaning upon famines of our own time. The word of Joseph becomes a word of God to us. Not one country, but every nation, "the haves" and "the have-nots" alike, know the agonizing specter of famine. Scarcity in the midst of plenty, but not of the means of subsistence alone. There is a famine of security. How can anyone who is aware of conditions not feel the agony of it? The sheer madness of men driven by the specter of it; the irrational expedients adopted to end it; the pitiful plight of thousands supinely resigned to it. The problem of security for nations and for the individuals composing them is not simple, nor is the solution simple. Basic conditions of economic well-being must be fulfilled; vast schemes of reconstruction already initiated must be continued. Symptoms must not be confused with causes, nor can beautiful generalities avail without working blueprints, prepared and executed by competent builders. Nevertheless, there is one condition so obvious that it is strange we so easily forget it: security, conceived in national or personal terms, speaks to anxious and distraught men these solemn words: "Ye shall not see my face, except your brother be with you." To forget this principle is to commit what has been called the sin of impersonality. It is to rely too greatly upon abstractions or material entities as if these were living, responsible beings—economic forces, economic laws, trade expansion, in the sphere of commerce; guns, planes, lines of force, and the rest in the sphere of national defense. With these matters government and other associations of responsible citizens must deal, and with urgency. For Western civilization and for men everywhere this is an age of exceptional crisis. But where do we as individuals come in? We must see the situation and our duty primarily in terms not of things but of persons. What are unemployment, an inflationary economy, meager charity, regimentation, doing to individuals? What does war mean to fathers and sons, to mothers and daughters? As the late British King George VI

observed, "Over all nations is humanity." This, you see, is the
essential Christian emphasis. It is not a vague humanitarianism,
but the heart of deep religion. God who forever honored humanity by His incarnation in Jesus, has revealed Himself as the
Father of all men. In Christ we have a new relation to God; we
have free access to the Father. But He is the Father of all, and
solitary fellowship with Him is impossible. The human brotherhood is the corollary of the Divine Fatherhood. Never, thank God,
has Christianity wholly lost that insight, but the magnitude of
present-day needs tends to daunt us. We may be honestly moved
by the plight of our fellows, and frightened by the possibilities
for ourselves. Do we return to our own country, and silence the
voice which recalls us to our task: "Ye shall not see the face of
security in your own nation, in your own community, and domestic life, except your brother accompany you, unless he know also
the meaning of being wanted, of self-respect, of personal significance"? Democracy at its creative best owes most to the Christian
faith. Himself a Conservative, the late Earl Baldwin quoted with
approval the famous sentence of Colonel Rainsboro to Cromwell:
"Really I think the poorest 'he' that is in England hath a life to
live as the richest 'he.'" He might have added: and the richest
"he" cannot live his life in serenity and joy unless he has sought
to insure for the "poorest he" the means of life worthy of the
name. In a lecture at the University of Toronto, the same English
statesman made these further observations:

> Democracies must attain to new levels of technical efficiency
> for self defence and learn to cooperate; . . . the countries they
> are called upon to defend with their lives must be in the eyes
> of their citizens more and more worth living and dying for,
> because they provide more and more the conditions and the
> elements of the good life—the divine right of the common
> man. . . . In other words, they must strive with more insistence
> and passion than ever before to make real the twin ideals of
> social justice and individual freedom. These are the pillars
> essential for the support of any decent civilization, Christian
> or other. . . .[1]

Would any Christian dissent? Yet we may be enamored of noble principles and indifferent to practical local application of them. Just before the war, a useful and honored member of the British House of Commons told of an acquaintance who was always talking about the Empire. He attended every Empire rally, joined every Empire league. Every proposal for the enlargement of the Empire he applauded with vigor. At breakfast, dinner, tea, he expatiated upon the glories of Empire. Unfortunately, compared with the imperial visions he cherished, his home appeared to him a restricted, depressing place. He treated his long-suffering and hard-working wife with some impatience. One day he arrived home before dinner was ready. The baby had been fretful; everything had gone wrong. "The imperial brow clouded, and there was thunder and lightning. The poor wife winced and wept beneath the storm; and then, smiling through her tears, she went towards her lord, laid the peevish baby in his arms, and said: 'There, now, you mind *your little bit of empire*, whilst I dish the potatoes!' " The praise and quest of security in general is praiseworthy; it is just possible the first step toward averting the famine is to do our part toward those nearest us, whether they be near kinsmen or not. In nearly every community, there are persons who will remain displaced and dispirited unless someone takes seriously the example and commands of Jesus. *"Ye shall not see my face, except your brother be with you."*

Today we confront another type of famine, *a famine of inward peace.* Does not the immense sale of books promising to provide peace of mind, peace of soul, confidence for living, underscore this fact? More companions on the human road than we think, are asking with William Cowper, some wistfully, others in quiet desperation:

> Where is the blessedness I knew
> When first I saw the Lord?

or, where is the blessedness others know? Here again, there may be several reasons for our restlessness and harassed, fugitive living. We fail to expose ourselves regularly and patiently to the healing sunshine of the Spirit in prayer, in worship, in meditation. Or we may be unwilling to tear the dearest idol we have known from the throne which belongs to the Lord of all. Self may have banished Christ. Or, it may be that we refuse to face up to what the Bible bluntly calls sin. We have tried to bury it, forget it, and it just refuses to stay decently interred. But sin, however abstract in name and theological definition, is no abstraction. It is something done to a *person*. "Father I have sinned against heaven and before *Thee*. . . ." We may have sought to fulfill various important conditions, and yet God seems unreal, and the peace which passeth understanding eludes us. So we may abandon our interior quest. As a kind of solution we busy ourselves with doing good to others. As another has said, many could confess, "I can never be the man I wanted to be. I set out with high ideals, but they are beyond me. I've struggled for long against besetting sin. Now I'll give up the struggle as hopeless. But I'll throw myself into the service of God." We are like a little boy who has quarreled with his brother. The mother does not punish, but her eyes are sad. The little lad is anxious to have things right. "Mummy, can I do anything for you? Can I get you something?" He gets her a present. It helps, but does not quite work. At last he runs to his brother and makes it up, says he's really sorry. Then he takes himself to his mother's arms and whispers, "Mummy, forgive me!" What did Jesus say about grievances toward others, and grievances others have toward us? "If therefore thou art offering thy gift at the altar and there rememberest that thy brother hath aught against thee, leave there thy gift before the altar; first be reconciled to thy brother and then come and offer thy gift."[2] Let me say it again, old and commonplace that it is, for it needs saying and believing and realizing: *"There is no such thing as a private reconciliation with God as long as relationships with men are not as right as we can make them."* The only petition in the Lord's Prayer to which any condition is attached is the prayer for forgiveness. "Ye shall not see My face," says the

God and Father of Jesus, who is our Father, "except your brother be with you."

Some years ago, a pathetic story of two nuns was published. These "sisters" were Bernardines who lived side by side in two adjoining cells, and so thin a partition divided them that they could even hear each other's breathing. All this time they ate at the same table and prayed in the same chapel. At last one of them died. According to the rule of the Order, the dead nun's body was laid in the chapel, her face uncovered. The sisters filed past, throwing holy water upon the remains as they went. When her next-door neighbor walked past, a startling thing occurred. No sooner did she catch sight of the dead nun's face than she gave a shriek and fainted. She had just recognized her dearest friend in the world, from whom she had parted in anger years before. Each had misunderstood the other, and thought the other unaffected by the quarrel. For five years the two friends had lived side by side in cloistered isolation, neither having seen the other's face nor heard the other's voice. Such tragedy is not fiction. Friends move asunder on paths that diverge more widely as the seasons creep into years, because the condition of reconciliation with God and with each other is not fulfilled. What pain it must bring to our blessed Lord that His own followers fail so lamentably in intimate personal relations! Too frequently, we suspect our fellow worshipers because they find help in ways alien to us. We isolate ourselves from the great movements of service we might share together because we have not tried to understand the motives and temperaments of others. "We are like islands and we shout to each other across seas of misunderstanding."

> O God! that men would see a little clearer,
> Or judge less harshly where they cannot see!
> O God! that men would draw a little nearer
> To one another!—they'd be nearer Thee,
> And understood.[3]

Friend, will you act upon this truth before the sun goes down on another day of misunderstanding? You *could* write a letter, if you cannot do the better thing: go directly to the person involved in that old misunderstanding or quarrel. You remind me that it may be of no use. It is quite possible that your overture may be rejected. But there is One who was despised and rejected of men, who did not give up, even on a Cross. He was always building bridges across chasms of enmity, suspicion and misunderstanding. His greatest bridge was in the form of a Cross. Those who walk that way, even with painful steps and slow, report a marvelous experience of the peace of God which comes *with* understanding. The only absolute essential in Christian behavior is Christlikeness. How can we ever attain even a little of that grace if we do not follow Him in this? No vision of God is vouchsafed the most earnest seeker so long as he refuses to clasp the hand of another whom he has excluded from the circle of his love. "We know that we have passed from death to life, because we love the brethren." "Ye cannot see My face, except your brother be with you."

Thus we stand face to face with Christ. We call Him Lord and Saviour. So He is! He is also our Elder Brother, who stooped to our humanity, the first born among many brethren. He reveals Himself as He is as we stand and as we serve linked with our brother. Somehow without Him we cannot see the face and heart of God. But He is with us, if we do not exclude Him by our lovelessness. In His companionship, and in His service, there is no dearth of security, or joy and peace; no lack of the glory of God. Why is it so? President Charles W. Eliot of Harvard, whose influence upon education and public life was immeasurable, carried a disfiguring birthmark which covered almost all of one side of his face. He seemed completely unconscious of it. One day he came upon a group of boys badgering one of their comrades. Instantly Dr. Eliot saw that the boy bore a birthmark and that this was the target of his companions' cruelty. Dr. Eliot drove the tormentors away. He then took the little lad and held him at arm's length and said, "Look, my boy, my face is marred, too." By his compassion and understanding he transcended his own sensitiveness and lifted the boy's morale. He saw the little ragamuffin as

a human being, with trials and sufferings like his own. You may
be sure the lad saw in his champion one like unto himself, but
mightier. We turn to One whose face was "marred more than
any man's." He takes His place beside us, links arms with us. We
are healed of all self-despising, of all uncertainty and fear. We
find God not in "the flight of the alone to the Alone," but most
near, most savingly, through Jesus Christ our Lord. We look,
however dimly, upon the Face of the ineffable God because our
Brother is with us.

PRAYER: *Holy Father, we are not worthy to be called thy sons. Yet
we come to Thee, for there is none other who can give us the Bread
of Life without which our souls hunger and die. Draw us nearer to
Thyself by drawing us nearer to one another, whatever our differences. Through the days when we are absent from one another,
keep us in Thy Love, and since we are not of ourselves able to live
the life we seek, give us the grace of our Lord Jesus Christ. Amen.*

9
Religion without Tears

It is too much for you to go up to Jerusalem.   1 KINGS 12:28 (R.S.V.)
. . . He would go to Jerusalem.   LUKE 9:53

W HAT many of us want is a religion without tears. New Testament Christianity demands too much. A shrewd king who
lived before the time of Christ saw that the high religion of the
Old Testament was too exacting. His name was Jeroboam, and he
ruled over one of the divided kingdoms. He was opposed to
reunion of Judah and Israel, and he noted with concern that the
devout citizens of his own realm continued to go up to Jerusalem
to Solomon's temple to worship God. He would provide churches
for them nearer their own homes. "It is too much for you to go
up to Jerusalem," said the king. "Let me provide temples for you
at Dan and Bethel, complete with gods and all other appur-
tenances. Jerusalem is a long and tiresome journey. Think how
unpleasant it is in bad weather! You work hard all week, and
then have to travel that great distance just because you met God
in Solomon's temple."

How considerate it was of the king! Or was it? Actually he was
far from being generous to his subjects; he was afraid that worshiping together might unite Judah and Israel once more, that the
breach of the two kingdoms might be healed, and that he would
lose his privileges and even his life. The Biblical historian makes
this terse comment on Jeroboam's action: "This thing became a
sin." This encouragement of a more comfortable religion became
a sin because it encouraged division, disunity and idolatry. Alexander Whyte observed truly that "all who divide, and keep

80

divided, nations and churches, and families, and friends, in order to make a name or a living, or a party . . . they are the true seed of Jeroboam."

Yes, Jeroboam offered to make religion easy, but a dark purpose to divide the household of faith was behind it. The devil, whatever his name, seeks to divide and rule.

I

"It is too much for you to go up to Jerusalem." This solicitude of the ancient kinglet for his subjects reminds us of a common temptation. In the most mature person there is a streak of softness to which this kind of suggestion makes an appeal. One of the most popular cults is the cult of the comfortable. It is unpleasant to be told that achievement in any field of interest requires self-denial, self-discipline; that the enduring prizes of life must be paid for in toil and sweat and sometimes the sacrifice of innocent pleasures. To scorn delights and live laborious days is for moral heroes. It may be that the original deposit of inertia has grown as a result of being compelled to live on "short rations" during the days of global war. Understandably many of us in North America hope that we can move into a more upholstered age. Why can't we be good to ourselves for a while? After all, we have poured men and treasure into Europe and Asia. It is unfortunate that they are hungry over there, but they asked for it, did they not? Yes, "it is too much for us to go up to Jerusalem"—the Jerusalem of continuing sacrificial service on behalf of the multitudes in dire need of our help.

As for making the long, painful trek to the Jerusalem of a truly united and functioning United Nations organization, well, perhaps the planet has shrunk so that we need a global strategy to handle it; but the Russians are impossible, the British are stubborn, and all the other countries don't help very much! "It is too much for us to go up to Jerusalem," for the trail takes it out of us in thinking and acting intelligently and with world-mindedness. If we have to rough it, let us rough it smoothly!

But at our best we know that such specious argument is the devil's own line. That strategem is satanic. We are children of a great God who gives Himself utterly, at incredible cost, to rescue us from the death of the soul. "The whole creation groaneth and travaileth in pain until now" to bring forth in us the qualities of wisdom, and kindness, and intelligence which the Father of our spirits seeks to develop in every member of His human family.

II

"It is too much for you to go up to Jerusalem." Is it? Well, going up to Jerusalem makes available *the saving insights, the transforming power and abiding joy of great religion.* This Lenten season challenges our mood of comfortableness. For in these weeks Christians of every denomination follow in reverent devotion the pilgrimage of Jesus. That sad and yet triumphant journey by the Son of God to Calvary and beyond tells us that we cannot have a great religion, a truly abundant life, without tears. Our Master is the Master of Joy, but it is the joy that one enters through the acceptance of a Cross. Multitudes find this Gospel not a little revolting. It may be that certain branches of the Church do emphasize the actual physical sufferings of Christ in such a manner as to be morbid. Nevertheless, in spite of excessive and crude representations of the sufferings and death of our Lord, Christendom has obeyed a sound impulse in making the Cross central.

A few years ago Aldous Huxley wrote a novel about the world of tomorrow. *Brave New World* he called it. It was certainly new! All harsh and cutting experiences of life have been magically canceled out. The intrusion of pain and trouble is unknown. The Controller, or chief director, of this Utopia proudly announces, "[It is] Christianity without tears." "But," cries another voice, "the tears are necessary. . . . You get rid of them. . . . You just abolish the slings and arrows. It's too easy. . . . I don't want comfort. I want God, I want poetry, I want real danger, I want freedom, I want goodness, I want sin." "In fact," says the Controller, "you're claiming the right to be unhappy." "All right then," retorts the other, "I'm claiming the right to be unhappy."[1] Somehow we feel that the protest is basically sound.

The Church of Christ proclaims, therefore, not an old or a new asceticism, but that there is no crown without a cross; no gain without pain. You ask me why? I can say only, It just is like that! And Christianity faces us with the fact of it, wriggle and squirm as we may.

Of course, the majority of casual people do not approve. If only Christ or His representatives would pitch the demands a little lower. Once in the wilderness, you remember, Christ was tempted to cast Himself down from the high peak of loyalty. Once again, in the wilderness of Pain the same temptation came: "Come down from the Cross!" As another said, "Pain, anguish, sorrow, doubt, darkness, the sense of being forsaken by God—these are the very last sensations, surely, that a son of God should ever know. So the thought came to our Lord. . . . If you are really the Christ you had better come down out of that if you expect us or anyone else to believe in you . . . to take the pain out of life and the sting out of sin, would that not be a sure way to the hearts of men? But He who hung and suffered there was as though He heard them not."[2] The same clamorous voice is heard today. So many will run sentimentally to Bethlehem who at Calvary "stand afar off beholding that sight," a bit disgusted and repelled by it all.

There are comfortable words of Christ, and many Roman Catholics, Protestants, Jews are familiar with them. These comfortable words bring healing and hope to many. Are we as familiar with the uncomfortable words of Christ? "What do ye more than others?" "If ye love Me, keep My commandments." "If any man would be My disciple, let him deny himself, take up his cross daily, and follow Me." "Go ye into all the world and make disciples af all nations." "Love your enemies, Forgive. . . ." If ever you are tempted to think of Christ as offering an easy kind of life, as being compassionate in a soft kind of way, recall what the first disciples said of His teaching: "Many therefore of His disciples, when they had heard this, said, This is an hard saying; who can hear it?"[3] Dean Sperry of Harvard suggests that one of the reasons many scientific friends take so little interest in churches and Christianity is that our portrayal of Christianity is too "soft" for them. "We preach a saccharine, spineless gospel of easygoing good nature. Our world is 'sweet,' while the universe with which they deal is rocky, reliable, but relentless, and if not bitter then certainly astringent."[4]

Who was it that said, "Enter ye in at the strait gate . . . because strait is the gate, and narrow is the way, which leadeth unto life?" ("The gate is narrow and the way is hard, that leads to life, and those who find it are few."[5])

It is not that anyone seriously believes that you reach the God and Father of Jesus by a process of self-torture! Christ's way for us is not a way of negation, but of affirmation. But the Gospel is harsh in its treatment of all that gets in the way of spiritual health and the soul's vision. We do have to renounce some things for the one thing that matters most.

Life seems woven about the principle of the Cross. Do you remember that strange story of the construction gang directed to erect a broadcasting station on the site of an old stone cross? The wrecking crew tried every ordinary means and the cross would not budge. Finally a spectator shouted, "They can't pull it over. They can't dig it up. It's from the beginning. It's the core of creation."

"It is too much for you to go to Jerusalem." That is a temptation which appeals to the softness in us. When it prevails in religion it reduces religion's purity and power. Indeed, whenever an individual or group clamors for a type of Christianity which is merely sweet and consoling, you are dealing, said Dr. Fosdick once out of many years in the ministry, "with somebody in process of deterioration."

It costs to reclaim a personality. It costs to rebuild a community without insecurity, without delinquency, without unwholesome institutions and practices. It costs to fashion a world structure for an enduring peace . . . But *a costly way of living can be re-*

demptive. One king said to his subjects, "It is too much for you to go to Jerusalem." Another King said to His subjects: "The Son of Man must go to Jerusalem." There was no other way to save the world. He *would* go up, says Luke. He had counted the cost. He knew there was no other way to effect the miracle of forgiveness and reconciliation; to placard before our eyes the holy love of God.

Sometimes in the church I served in a Canadian city, I would enter the building when it was empty of other human beings. Seated in a back pew, I would look up to the chancel window with its impressive reproduction of Holman Hunt's painting, "The Light of the World." Then my eyes would rest upon the cross placed on the holy table. The replica of Christ's cross seemed to grow brighter as I moved slowly toward the chancel. Is that why the old Gospel hymn had us sing, "Jesus, keep me near the Cross," so that we should be challenged, arrested, compelled to move out of our indifference and comfort? This sentence by one of our informed Christian leaders is provocative: *"The history of Christianity could be written in terms of the ingenious and fatal ways in which Christians have tried to make their faith and practice easy."* You may not try to make your faith easy by substituting ritual for moral seriousness. You may not be guilty of making creedalism a substitute for working faith in God and man. But you and I may try to make our religion easy by "a negative, moderate morality." "What do ye more than others? Do not even pagans the same?" This is a hurt and desperate world. It will be saved only as men and women who believe in God and Christ and the Kingdom take some portion of the work of Christ upon their hearts and minds. The mark of the disciple is that we deny ourselves, take up our cross, and follow Him. What does the Cross mean for you? Dr. Clow of Glasgow once offered a helpful definition. In Scripture three words express with perfect insight the darker and more difficult experiences of the religious life. The three words are "burden," "thorn," and "cross." We frequently confuse them. *Burden* is used to describe the inevitable strain and cares of earthly life, our tasks, our duties, our responsibilities. These we can bear steadfastly only as we cast them on Him who is able to give us strength to bear our own burdens. By *"thorn"* we mean the experience of a keener anguish, some singular trial, some humbling infirmity, some mortifying disability. The thorn may be some affliction in our dearest. We do not name it, and we accept it successfully in the power of the divine grace. The third word is *cross*. There is a sense in which we can speak truly of the inevitability of the Cross. But concerning our own cross there is a sense in which it is escapable. Many refuse to carry it. "Soft-lapped in luxury" they find the cross nasty, unpleasant. A cross is something more than we commonly mean by the word. You remember the English girl who surprised her employer by saying, "The lady worker says, madam, that you are my cross." Jesus had his *burden*; his subjection to the conditions of human existence, toil, poverty, weariness and pain. He had his *thorn*. No one knows what it may have been. Perhaps His sensitive mind, under the pressure of the world's coarse hand, and the horror of the world's evil, composed His thorn. He had His *Cross*. He took it up. He might have laid it down. At His baptism He laid it on His shoulders. In His temptation He bound it to Him with cords. His Cross was that life and death for sinful men and women which came to consummation in His dying hour. Your cross? It is something you take or refuse. It may be some special burden of the cares of others, or of the service of your fellows. It may be some share in poverty or privation which you could escape by taking a lower course. It may be some refusal of place or power or love for conscience' sake. "It is surely to live chastely in an impure world, to be just and true and loving to those who scorn you, to care for the glory of God above everything else, to lay your powers on the altar of sacrifice to Christ, and to follow Him cost what it may."[6] O men and women who would serve the will of God, who would make this a saner and lovelier earth for your children and successors: we cannot have the personal life, the community and the world of our best dreams without the Cross. We cannot have the

Church we seek without sacrifice. We have not yet given to the point of blood. We have not yet faced hardship and hostility for our faith and fellowship in Christ. May this not be the reason why His Kingdom advances so slowly among us? The common assertion that Christianity has failed to find the cure for the ills of mankind is usually countered by saying that Christianity has not failed, it has not been tried. Well, mankind has tried Christianity, but it has not tried it hard enough. "Neither will I offer . . . unto the Lord my God of that which cost me nothing."[7] Is it too much for you to go to Jerusalem? You may stay at home in your Dan or Bethel. These are less exacting shrines. You may keep your religion for inner personal attitudes only. But if you will not go up you will miss the Lord of Glory. And you will miss that dear City of God because every approach to the City of the redeemed is the result of a surrendered will, an accepted cross, a life somehow laid down. The old phrase remains true: no cross, no crown. Bishop Crotty of Australia told of a sixteen-year-old girl dying in one of England's great hospitals. She had been the eldest child in a large, poor family. Her mother had died when the youngest child was born, and for years she had spent her girlhood bearing the burdens of a home and mothering the younger children. She had been literally tired to death and was dying of tuberculosis. Her face was white and drawn. Her hands were rough with the work of years. Round the wards came a lady visitor of a type we sometimes describe as pious or unco guid; a person of extremely conventional and narrow outlook. The visitor questioned the patient about religion. Had she been confirmed? No. Had she been baptized? No! Had she gone to Sunday School? No, she had never had time for that. The questions went on, and all were answered with a weary "No." The lady visitor took a serious view of it all. "What will you do," she asked, "when you die, and have to tell God that?" The girl who had given herself for others in daily hard work, who had gone doggedly on to her Jerusalem and was now moving through Gethsemane and Calvary in the suburbs of the heavenly Jerusalem, laid two transparent,

work-stained hands on the coverlet. She lifted to her questioner
big, dark, glowing eyes, full of peace. Then she made answer too
sublime for comment. Very quietly she whispered, "I will show
Him my hands."

> Show me Thy hands, O Christ—but not the marred
> Poor broken hands that, piteously held out,
> Are love's last argument to silence doubt.
> With those Thou openest heav'n, to me not barred,
> Since I believe; the meanwhile is more hard—
> In this world's common ways, to be about
> The Father's business! Leave me not without
> Thine own life-pattern clear to my regard.

PRAYER: *O Saviour, who didst set Thy face as a flint to go to Jerusalem to Thy Cross and Passion, help us, Thy weak and wavering
disciples, to be firm and resolute in the path of duty. We confess
that we have refused to share the burden of Thy Cross, that we
have denied Thee rather than face mockery, and have sought comfort and security rather than the doing of Thy will. Forgive our
sin, help us to amend, and give us courage to endure worthily; for
Thy Name's sake. Amen.*

10
Heartbreak Hill

So Jesus also suffered outside the gate in order to consecrate the people through his own blood. Therefore let us go forth to Him outside the camp, bearing abuse for Him.   HEBREWS 13:12, 13 (R.S.V.)

FIERCE conflict and human sacrifice invest place names with lasting fame or infamy. When the issue of a particular struggle proves of decisive importance to the combatants, the area of fighting itself becomes part of the collective memory. So the names of once unknown hills or valleys, islands or villages, possess the familiarity of places near at hand. Few of us may be able to recite the names of history's decisive battles, but all recognize many of them when we hear them. Select a few at random and see if it is not true. Thermopylae, Waterloo, Gettysburg, Verdun, Dunkirk, Warsaw, Corregidor, and—for many who lived through World War II—names of beachheads, little islands in the Pacific, have power to evoke various emotions. True, many places once considered unforgettable are remembered now only by historians or veterans of the wars. For the majority Wordsworth's line describes their present significance:

old, unhappy, far-off things,
And battles long ago.

Such may be the fate of one section of terrain in Korea. In the opening years of the second half of the twentieth century, however, few in the Western world do not know the name Heartbreak Ridge, or Heartbreak Hill. On that now jagged ridge line overlooking the Mundung Valley thousands of men from Communist and from United Nations forces fought the most savage action of

89

the Korean War. Thousands were wounded and more thousands were killed. A wounded young American soldier is credited with giving the name. After being carried to his own lines he described the place and the struggle in simple, poignant words. "It's a heartbreak," he cried, "it's a heartbreak." The name remained. Edith Lovejoy Pierce views Heartbreak Ridge with Christian realism in her lines:

> Men die
> To an accompaniment of aimless chatter—
> Drag themselves slowly up a hill
> While an imaginary line is drawn on a map.
> Talks have been resumed,
> But pain has never ceased.
> No one will give an inch
> When a world is being saved
> Or lost.
> The human heart
> Is always bleeding to death on a hill
> While somebody trumps an ace
> Or dices for outer garments.[1]

Nineteen hundred years ago there was an earlier Heartbreak Hill. "Jesus also suffered" a cruel death on a hill. On that skull-shaped hill outside a city wall, history's most decisive battle reached its climax. Heartbreak Hill in Korea and the hill called Calvary in Palestine both dramatize the human tragedy. Calvary dramatizes and demonstrates much more.

Have you ever thought of the crucifixion of Christ as a disclosure of the basic nature of our human situation? Surely in the suffering and death of the holiest and best at the hands of men like ourselves we see that *conflict between good and evil is real and deep and deadly.* Long before perceptive analysts of human relationships declared it to be so, Biblical writers insisted that to be human is to be engaged in a constant battle. Psychologists tell us that personality is a battlefield, with the will to live fighting for supremacy over the destructive impulse. Certainly it is romantic to deny the existence of what the apostle Paul called "fightings within." Who does not know from firsthand experience that the soul is the scene of an inward civil war? In a world of persons, does not the growing child do battle for the self he feels is his and which he senses is jeopardized by the imperialistic designs of the adults in his world? As for the life we live in the larger world, mutual aid confronts mutual competition. Life may not be wholly a battle for survival, but it frequently looks like it. Like it or not, we face evil—militant, aggressive and pervasive. In a developing world, in which the human inhabitants have the dangerous and precious gift of freedom, conflict is present. Individual and group wills clash, and contending forces struggle for the mastery. Paul's reading of the facts may be unwelcome; it is more adequate than our more optimistic interpretations. "For we are not contending against flesh and blood, but against the principalities, against the powers, against the world rulers of this present darkness, against the spiritual hosts of wickedness in the heavenly places."[2]

This is how it is for the Christian, says the apostle. When you enlist under Christ's banner, and seek to make Him Lord over all of life, you are asking for it. When Christians move out into the field of action they can count on stirring up the forces of hate and malignancy.

If you would know the intensity of this conflict and its critical character, get you to Heartbreak Hill, where "Jesus also suffered" from the worst that men could do. "Consider Him who endured from sinners such hostility against Himself, so that you may not grow weary or faint-hearted."[3] Aye, consider Him, lest you yield to the illusion that the devilish elements in the picture are imaginary or at least exaggerated by gloomy theologians. "Have you found peace, brother?" an evangelist once asked a redoubtable champion of human freedom. "No," retorted the other, "I have found war." Abraham Lincoln has been called one of America's profound and original theologians by no less a person then Reinhold Niebuhr. At least Lincoln grasped the deep truth of the matter when he said, "There is no ground between right and wrong, except battle-ground." At Golgotha, as we gaze at the broken Figure on the central cross, we know that it is a fight to the finish.

In this critical conflict you and I are inextricably involved. Somehow, the dreadful act of the crucifiers moves out of Palestine and the first century into our community and time. By our willful wrongdoing, by our betrayal of the best, by our moral failures in intimate relationships and in the larger social context in which we move, we "crucify the Son of God afresh, and put him to an open shame." The forces of truth and love and justice have landed on the territory occupied by the hosts of darkness, and often we have slunk from the field. Is it too much to say that by our easy tolerance of evil we have on occasion acted as collaborationists with the enemy?

> Three crosses stood on Calvary
> Stark against the sky.
> Roman soldiers laughed to see
> Three ways a man may die.
>
> Crosses still stand on Calvary
> Stark again the sky,
> And some still laugh to see
> Men die . . . hear little children cry.
>
> Who builds the cross on Calvary
> Stark against the sky?
> Who laughs at pain and want?
> Can it be you—or I?[4]

"I would think the evil of the world would break God's heart," a man once said to a Christian leader. "It did," was the quiet reply. Calvary is God's Heartbreak Hill. "God so loved the world that He gave His only Son," wrote John in his Gospel. Just because God is love, He could no other. But the sin which made the Cross inevitable broke His heart. Do we not find here the reason why the death of a Man nineteen centuries ago exerts strange power over us? Is it not because we at least dimly perceive that the death of Christ is more than a martyrdom? That in ways which baffle our thought and speech to define, God Himself was in Christ, in His life, and in His sacrificial death?

Somewhere these lines were printed. Their author's name is Barbara Harbert.

> "The key to a whole campaign
> Is often the top of a lonely hill,"
> The major said.
>
> I thought, How true!
> The Key to all our love and hope,
> All our joy and kindness,
> All our forgiveness and faith
> Was found nineteen hundred years ago
> On the top of a lonely hill.

This is the claim of the Christian faith. It is a claim validated by the experience of innumerable men and women. These have found in the action on Christ's Heartbreak Hill and in its sequel in the resurrection of Christ, the key to the meaning of existence and the key which opens the door into the heart of God. The Cross is the key, or rather the Man on the Cross is the key to the whole campaign. As the ancient Christian hymn affirms,

> When Thou hadst overcome the sharpness of death,
> Thou didst open the Kingdom of Heaven to all believers.

Doubtless the author of the *Te Deum Laudamus* referred to Christ's gift of eternal life beyond this phase. By the divine action in Christ's death and resurrection, men and women who respond with their trust and love, find themselves here and now in the Kingdom of Heaven. For the Kingdom of God means "righteousness and peace and joy in the Holy Spirit."[5] His righteousness, His peace and His joy become ours in spite of what we are and have done. Here is the classical statement of the truth, as Paul set it down: "While we were yet helpless, at the right time Christ died for the ungodly. Why, one will hardly die for a righteous man—though perhaps for a good man one will dare even to die. But God shows His love for us in that while we were yet sinners

Christ died for us.''[6] God proves His love toward us, says Paul, establishes it, demonstrates it. He forgives us. He reconciles us to the reality we have opposed or sought to escape. Why are we sure? Because as Christ was in the days of His human life and in the hour of His dying, so God is eternally. As Peter said to the Jerusalem council before whom he stood as a prisoner: "The God of our fathers raised Jesus whom you killed. . . . God exalted Him at His right hand as Leader and Saviour, to give repentance to Israel and forgiveness of sins.''[7] The divine Christ is now forever one with the Christlike Father. To the penitent sinner He speaks through the Holy Spirit as long ago He spoke: "Thy sins are forgiven thee. Go into peace."

Is there someone here haunted by a bitter memory? You did something back there you would give anything to have undone. You have tried not to think about it, but like a gray ghost it keeps plaguing you. You were younger, less mature, you argue to yourself, and "what's ended can't be mended." The trouble is that you are not wholly convinced that it is ended; that the chain of consequences has been broken. You have resolved not to be morbid about it, and you certainly do not intend to become neurotic. And yet you would like to have it settled once and for all. Christ came to liberate every man, every woman, from the evil we do by being us. By His complete identification with God's purpose and with God's human family He turned the chain of evil consequences into a chain of good. It is on what John Bunyan called "the place ascending" that we know. On Heartbreak Hill, where sin broke the Redeemer's heart, we find our hearts mended, our sins forgiven, our hostility to God's purpose for us and for His children everywhere transformed into acceptance. Crucifixion followed by the resurrection convinces us that the last word is with divine love. God has vindicated the Man on the Cross and vindicated our highest hopes. "Therefore, if any one is in Christ, he is a new creation; the old has passed away, behold, the new has come. All this is from God.''[8] And it is for you. Martin Luther is said to have prized the pronouns in the Gospel. In the pronouns he found himself grasped by the truth of Christ. "This is My Body broken for *you*." "*He* loved *me*, and gave Himself for *me*." This is where it begins. This is where He begins. Forgiven, healed, restored, then we climb with Him to the levels of insight and service where we say "we" and "our," in terms of our social duties and human needs. "For the love of Christ controls us, because we are convinced that One has died for all; therefore all have died. And He died for all, that those who live might live no longer for themselves but for Him who for their sake died and was raised."[9]

> The Key to all our love and hope,
> All our joy and kindness,
> All our forgiveness and faith
> Was found nineteen hundred years ago
> On the top of a lonely hill.

Will you take the key and use it? He stands at the door of the soul's house, but as Holman Hunt's famous picture rightly emphasized, the handle and the lock are on our side.

There is a battle. The conflict is real. It is decisive, and becomes a decision for us to make that will shape our personal history and the future of many others. *On Heartbreak Hill there is also a victory*. This victory has been won, although in one sense its consummation is not yet. New Testament language makes this vivid and clear. "You, who were dead in trespasses . . . God made alive together with Him, having forgiven us all our trespasses, having canceled the bond which stood against us with its legal demands; this He set aside, nailing it to the cross. He disarmed the principalities and powers and made a public example of them, triumphing over them in Him."[10] An alternative translation of the last phrase points to the crucial battlefield: "triumphing over them in the cross."

One of the oldest and noblest of our Protestant communions is the Moravian Church. Recently it observed its five hundredth anniversary. Across the years the seal of the Moravian Church has carried the emblem of a lamb bearing a banner on which is the symbol of Calvary. Circling it round is the Church's motto,

Angus noster vicit; eum sequamur—"Our Lamb has conquered; let us follow Him." It is an inspiring confession and challenge. Does not the Bible declare that "He must reign until He has put all His enemies under His feet"?[11] Does not the book of vision also report the triumph accomplished "beyond history"? "The kingdom of the world has become the kingdom of our Lord and of His Christ, and He shall reign for ever and ever."[12]

On Heartbreak Hill on the first Good Friday, the conflict between truth and falsehood, good and evil, love and hatred reached its critical climax. On Heartbreak Hill in Palestine God's crucial self-disclosure as redemptive love was made. Where the heart of God in Jesus Christ was broken, our broken lives are mended. Where brutal force won a temporary victory, God came victor. "Jesus also suffered outside the gate in order to consecrate the people through His own blood. Therefore, let us go forth to Him outside the camp, bearing abuse for Him."

> Heart, are you great enough
> For a love that never tires?
> O heart, are you great enough for love?
> I have heard of thorns and briers.

PRAYER: *O Father of our Lord Jesus Christ, who didst graciously send thy Son to suffer and to die for us men and for our salvation, make us truly thankful for this unspeakably great gift. For Thy longsuffering with the sins and sorrows of Thy children from the beginning even until now; for the sufferings of Christ on the Cross and for His intercession for mankind in glory, we thank Thee. Above all, for the redemption of the world which Thou hast wrought through the pain of the Passion and the shame of the Cross, we thank Thee. Enable us by Thy grace to fill up the sufferings of Christ in our lives for love of Thee and for all for whom Christ died; so may we know Thee more clearly, love Thee more dearly and follow Thee more nearly, O Divine Redeemer. Amen.*

11

The Secret Society

You are permitted to know the secrets of the Kingdom of Heaven, but they are not.

MATTHEW 13:11 (Goodspeed)

All these things spake Jesus unto the multitude in parables; and without a parable spake he not unto them: That it might be fulfilled which was spoken by the prophet, saying, I will open my mouth in parables; I will utter things which have been kept secret from the foundation of the world.

MATTHEW 13:34-35

Yet there is a wisdom that we impart when we are with people who have a mature faith . . . it is a mysterious divine wisdom that we impart, hitherto kept secret, and destined by God before the world began for our glory.

1 CORINTHIANS 2:6, 7 (Goodspeed)

SECRET societies express an ancient and widespread interest of man. One of the institutions of primitive society was called the Men's House, "a secret lodge in which every young man, when he came to maturity, was initiated into the law, legend, and tradition of his people." In the formative period of human society these secret lodges played an important part in developing a sense of kinship, sanctity and loyalty which lies at the roots of law, order and religion.

Boys and girls enjoy belonging to secret clubs, and when they become young adults in school and college often devote much time and energy to fraternities, even as their fathers do to their fraternal associations.

Have you ever considered the Church of Christ as the great Secret Society of the ages? Of course it is the Society of the *Open* Secret. Whosoever will may come into its mystic brotherhood, provided he or she comes with sincerity and love. Of course this secret order of the disciples of Christ does not deal in what is called *esoteric* wisdom. Esoteric means that which relates the

97

inner, hidden meaning of doctrine or philosophy, teaching which is handed down by secret tradition among the initiated. Commonly the ritual and teaching of fraternal orders could be called esoteric, reserved for a privileged few. The blessed Founder of our Great Society, Jesus our Master, declared Himself to be the Light of the *world*, not of an exclusive company. Of His movement it was early said, "This thing was not done in a corner." Nevertheless, He founded the Society of the Open Secret. Listen to Him, as Matthew reports His saying: "You are permitted to know the secrets of the Kingdom of Heaven, but they are not."[1] He was speaking to His followers, to the initiated. Later in the same chapter, Matthew tells us this is why Jesus spoke to the crowd in parables. As a prophet foretold, the Messiah uttered "things which have been kept secret from the foundation of the world."

What is the secret around which this ancient, invincible society is built? It is called "the precious secret" of Jesus, His secret of the life that is life indeed. St. Paul would call it the life here and hereafter "in Christ," with Christ's spirit and Christ's law dominating. It is the secret of absolute trust toward God, the Christlike Father; undiscouraged good will toward our fellow men; and strictest honesty with ourselves—our weaknesses and strengths, our defeats and victories, our obligations and privileges.

The secret contains "the pattern for dynamic behavior." The principles of this pattern are expounded in what we called the Beatitudes. The dynamic itself is found in companionship with the Crucified and Risen Lord within the communion or fellowship of His holy Spirit which we call the holy catholic Church.

Today, we are to receive into this "secret" Society of Jesus the candidates who present themselves after their course of instruction. Each of them has been "initiated." The initiation, or first gateway into the Order, is called Christian Baptism. Some received it in infancy, vows being then pledged for them by their parents. Some received Baptism in more mature years, taking the vows for themselves and consciously receiving Christ's approval and the assurance of His help in remaining His faithful servants unto life's end.

Today therefore marks a profoundly significant period in the life of every initiate who desires to be confirmed in the Faith and admitted to all the rights and privileges, all the obligations and sacrifices of Full Membership.

For a few minutes, on behalf of your comrades here and everywhere, and in the spirit of Him who is our Supreme Head—the Master of the divine lodge—let me remind you of certain features of this Society into which you ask to be received.

It is an *ancient* society. No other organization can boast of such a long continuous history. It goes back across nineteen centuries to Pentecost, sometimes called the Birthday of the Church. But it goes back behind Pentecost to Calvary and the first Easter. Had Christ not died for us men and for our salvation and had He not risen again in spiritual power we should not be here. Yet in a deep sense the Church was not founded by our blessed Saviour so much as found by Him, given a new birth and direction and a dimension of life which has made it eternal. For Jesus was Himself a member of the Jewish church or society, with its roots far back and deep down in the dim beginnings of His people. Indeed the Church goes back to that remote day when primitive man first turned from the sod to the sky and joined with his brother and sister in acknowledging, however crudely, the reality of the Unseen and Eternal.

It is *a world-wide, inclusive society.* In every land there are members. You may discover such colleagues in spite of differences in speech, color, methods of worship and government, by the spirit which animates them, by the faith, hope and love which characterize their attitudes and activities. For this Order of the Followers of Jesus can never rest content with maintaining strong "chapters" or units at home. Its leaders and discerning members know that it must obey the marching orders of its Founder and go out into all the world "discipling" all nations.

It is inclusive. Sororities and fraternities sometimes encounter difficulty on campuses because of their exclusiveness. A few of these societies wrongly draw lines according to color or creed, race or religion. Because of a false emphasis upon the financial standing of members, they deprive poor but worthy students of the chance to belong. Sometimes in the wider community secret societies degenerate into political machines which threaten the health of a democratic society. But this Society of the precious secret of our Master is a regenerating force. Wherever members of this Order go with the "mysterious divine wisdom" of God in Christ, even ignorant and illiterate folk find life liberated and made richly meaningful. Christians keep communities from becoming putrid and rancid; they are the salt of the earth, the leaven in the lump which keeps the mass wholesome and sweet. Therefore when you unite with this Church or any other Christian church you unite with the greatest brotherhood the world knows. You do not need to have wealth or learning, although these can be greatly used for our Master's cause; nor does your color or background determine your fitness for membership. Birth's invidious bar is no barrier. As the Duke of Wellington said at the communion rail, "We are all alike here." All you need is a little love for Christ, a little trust—all you can muster may be meager—to give Him. "I have chosen you," He says—"in ways mysterious, unknown—and My resources—My grace—will be ample for your needs."

In all secret societies, ancient and modern, certain features are fairly common and constant. There is not only initiation, but there is *a new name, a new language of signs,* grips and tokens, whereby the member may make himself known to his fellows in the dark as well as in the light. By a kind of instinct men discovered that everything should not be told to everybody, that men and women should show themselves worthy to receive truths which had cost so much. Jesus once said to His close friends that He had many things to say to them which they could not receive but which they would be able to understand later. Yes, says Paul, "There is a wisdom that we impart when we are with people who have a mature faith. . . . it is a mysterious divine wisdom . . . hitherto kept secret, and destined by God before the world began for our glory." This wisdom is called elsewhere the unsearchable riches of Christ, the unsurpassed treasures which are made known to us as we keep close to Him through regular prayer, through the sacraments, through costly Christlike service. Once when an old pagan magistrate asked a Christian prisoner who was the god that Christians worshiped, he replied, "If thou art worthy thou shalt know." So you know, and will know as you keep worthy by your teachable, modest spirit—by your loyal fulfillment of the holy vows you take this day.

Is there *a new name*? Aye, you have it—your *Christian* name.

Is there a grip or special handclasp? Yes, it is the right hand of fellowship which you receive today from the Church and from our Leader's pierced hands. It is the hand outstretched to help some struggling pilgrim; it is the hand full of food, of money, of compassionate ministry toward those in need anywhere, whether they be of the household of faith or not.

What is the *Password*? It is *Christ,* another word for Love divine, all loves excelling.

> None other Lamb, none other Name,
> None other Hope in heaven or earth or sea . . .
> . . . None beside Thee.[2]

Is there *secret lore or wisdom*? Yes; for it is unknown to the ignorant, the flippant, the sophisticate. The secret lore by which we find wisdom to live in desperate or in sunny hours is within the old Book, the Bible. One Korean convert could recite the whole of the Sermon on the Mount. To a surprised missionary he gave the explanation: "At first I tried to commit it to memory verse by verse, but it would not stick. So I tried a new plan. I took just one little bit of the Sermon and said, 'Tomorrow I am going to try that on my neighbor.'"

Is there a secret sign? Aye, it is the Cross of our Lord and Saviour Jesus Christ. To others it is a stumbling block, a symbol of defeat, a badge of shame. To us who are being saved it is the power of God, the dynamic of new life. This sign is as high as heaven, as deep as hell, as wide as the world in its need. We are signed with this Cross. It marks the limit of the service to which we are called. And in a sense we write our names in our lifeblood even as God in Christ wrote His name in blood on Calvary—God, His mark—making the New Covenant. In that masterpiece of early English literature, *The Vision of Piers Plowman,* William Langland refers to Calvary and says:

> Blood-brothers did we all become there
> And gentlemen each one.

Is there *a ritual meal?* Yes: it is the Sacrament of the Lord's Supper. In this lasting Supper we find Christ Himself the Host and we His unworthy guests. Through the symbols of broken bread and outpoured wine within this worshiping company He gives Himself in spiritual presence and power. We renew our vows, and pledge our love and loyal service. He asks us to come. "It was the last thing He askit of His friends," said a simple Scottish girl who was asked by the kirk-session why she wished to take Communion.

What of the obligations we take upon ourselves? Do not look at us who have preceded you to discover what the obligations are! We fail so often, so miserably. Once we, too, promised to be Christ's faithful soldiers. Yet we neglected His orders, stopped reading the manual of our Order, treated the meetings of His people with casualness, and have been content to live a life no better, no worse than the average. But Christians are to be different, are to be disciplined, to be united with one another in the bonds of love; to live ahead of their time and above the average. The fellowship and service of fraternal orders and service clubs is their noblest resource and contribution. We, too, are within "the Fellowship of the Concerned."

Does it all sound formidable? Do you feel that you are simply unequal to such high, exacting requirements? If you do, there is hope! Heads may be lost in the warfare Christ's Church may have to wage with the forces of darkness; but never will hearts be lost which are committed to Him. It is a glorious adventure to which He calls you, calls us all. It is "an affair of cavalry to be dashingly hazarded." If you listen with your spirit as you kneel before the unseen Master of our Lodge you will hear the sound of invisible trumpets blowing to rally you to the long, arduous and thrilling campaign.

"*You*"— lucky you!—"you are permitted to know the secrets of the Kingdom of Heaven." As you keep close to our divine Lord and Leader He will impart to you His wisdom for living. Like the cavalier of Charles I, you will serve your King "with a constant, dangerous and expensive loyalty."

PRAYER: *O God the king of glory who hast marvelously called us to share the secrets of Thy realm, accept these thy children who now offer to Thee the service of their lives. Admit them and us, despite our unworthiness, to the Mind of Christ, that in all our thoughts and deeds we may glorify Thee and continue Christ's faithful soldiers and servants unto life's end. Daily increase in them and in us Thy manifold gifts of grace; the spirit of wisdom and understanding; the spirit of knowledge and true godliness; and keep us all in thy mercy unto life eternal; through Jesus Christ our Lord. Amen.*

12

I Saw Two Calvaries

And sitting down they watched Him there.   MATTHEW 27:36

EARLY in the year 1942 the first American troops to reach
England in World War II marched into London. Their
friendly invasion thrilled the admiring populace and exhilarated
the soldiers themselves. The Yanks had come! Gleefully they sang
from "deep in the heart of Texas," Maine, Michigan and nearly
every state in the Union. As they turned into one of the main
thoroughfares an unexpected hush fell over the marching men.
Jaunty songs and gay greetings died on their lips. For at that
moment they looked for the first time upon an area which had
been severely blitzed. Before their eyes gaped the great wounds
inflicted by aerial bombardment. With mute sympathy they
realized that this city and its people had suffered terribly.

Something like that overtakes a sensitive mind on Palm Sunday. On this first day of Holy Week the Christian Year takes
us on pilgrimage with Christ into the city near which He died
a violent and vicious death. The holiest week in Christian story
begins with a joyous and friendly invasion of the capital. The
divine liberator comes! But soon the cheers are stifled by sobs,
and by a strange compulsion mankind lingers not amid the palms
of triumph but beside that "jagged tree" of tragedy. Like the
soldiers of a vanished empire appointed to supervise His execution, we too take our places on Calvary. Somehow, on that skull-
shaped hill, vision is clarified, insight is sharpened, and we see
more deeply into the meaning of life.

What do you see as you sit and watch Him there? Those

American soldiers saw two Englands as they entered the old city. At first they saw relatively unscarred landscape and homes; then, turning a corner, they beheld some of the visible results of man's inhumanity to man.

Mr. H. V. Morton whose travel books have delighted us all, assured us that he too saw two Englands. There was the England he toured immediately preceding hostilities. It was placid and conventional. Compact of the ancient and the modern, of quiet homes and stately piles, of vast estates and sordid slums, it was the England most of us knew. The other England was the England of total war. Stern and demanding, desperate and daring, wounded but not in her courage, she lifted a symbol of something undying and heroic in the human spirit. "I saw two Englands," says Mr. Morton, and we detect pride and sadness in his voice.

"Behold, I show you a mystery"—the mystery of a twentieth-century man looking at the crucifixion of Christ, and beholding not one but two Calvaries. "The Christian Church," wrote Dr. John Knox,[1] "had its origin in a mystery, if not in a miracle; in the unexplained, if not in the inexplicable." Consider this mystery, that an event nineteen hundred years and continents distant from us possesses contemporaneous quality; that the crucifixion of the Galilean long ago seems reproduced in our own tortured generation; that something done in and through that death exercises present and personal influence upon you and me—upon all of us today.

I saw two Calvaries—one on

a green hill far away
Without a city wall,

and the other on this earth in the agony of war.

No reputable student of history denies the actuality of Jesus' death on the Cross. Nor, save in jaundiced minds, is there disagreement as to the causes of His summary execution. Corrupt politicians, proud and privileged ecclesiastics, a disillusioned revolutionary, a stupid and indifferent community conspired to accomplish His removal from a society He disturbed and challenged. The holiest became intolerable as He confronted an immoral society. The forces which hustled Him out of the city and up to Golgotha reside in us still. He compels a verdict; either we release Him or we crucify Him, and try to end forever His dream of a humanity redeemed.

Thus, it is not fanciful but starkest realism to see the reproduction of Calvary throughout the world today. If another global war is in the making, it is because of global evil, and planetary guilt ultimately traces its slimy path to our doors.

Can an honest man deny that the fairest and best endures crucifixion everywhere in the world? Barbarism has donned the whole armor of science and defiled the sanctities earlier generations believed to be inviolable. Not easily will I forget the bitter contempt for fellow men of another nation which cut through the speech of Frank Laskier, a merchant seaman whose ship encountered a lifeboat from a torpedoed passenger ship in the North Atlantic. His skipper had the boat hoisted onto the deck. When the sailors lifted the tarpaulin, they saw the frozen bodies of little children who had died from exposure after their refugee ship, *City of Benares,* had been sunk. That crucifixion of the innocent did something to Laskier. He took a solemn vow that he would not rest until he had done his utmost on any of the seven seas to expel the monstrous evil that had caused it. To the long list of destroyed ships you may add such names as Czechoslovakia, Warsaw, Rotterdam, Lidice, Greece, Pearl Harbor; yes, Cologne, Bremen, Rostov, Lübeck, Hiroshima, Korea along with the others whose epitaphs modern man has written in flame.

Granted, that in this era there seems no alternative but to practice an "interim ethic" in so devilish a world; that now we must by force limit the area of infection lest we lose forever the chance to try for a saner system of relationships. Nevertheless *"mea culpa"* is the authentic cry of honest souls who see this second Calvary of our own creation. It will not do now to mouth the easy speeches of superficial men, and murmur our pained regrets over this temporary relapse into dark ages. Your modern pagan may be dubious about schemes of salvation, but he has no doubts left about the need for salvation.

You may remember that Studdert-Kennedy stumbled over an "undersized, underfed German boy, with a wound in his stomach and a hole in his head," and he saw another Calvary.

> From that moment on I have never seen the world as anything but a Crucifix. I see the cross set up in every slum, in every filthy overcrowded quarter, in every vulgar flaring street that speaks of luxury and waste of life. I see him staring up at me from the pages of the newspaper that tells of a tortured, lost, bewildered world.[2]

"And sitting down they watched Him there," with the earth for His Calvary and all men His crucifiers.

I saw two Calvaries—one at the center of Christian faith; the other in the heart of God. That Swedish saint, the late Archbishop Söderblom, summed up the significance of the Cross in Christian experience when he wrote, "The horrible spectacle of one crucified as a criminal is the central point in the highest religious worship of the human race." In Christian belief the Cross is central. It is the supreme symbol of faith because through it the highest speaks to the deepest in man, and speaks the one solving Word of God man most needs to receive. Calvary finds us at our worst and evokes our best, as no other event in history has power to do. A few shining Apollos may deny their need of a Saviour; most of us have learned through shame and sorrow that if we are to be recovered to moral health and spiritual wholeness Another must participate with us in that miracle.

True, our Lord's life and teaching provide essential elements in the process of our remaking and re-education. Yet, in the deed done on Calvary power is released which breaks the heart and mends it. Unveiled before our eyes, we see the reality of sin and the remedy for this essential wrongness in our human nature.

When Socrates lay dying his friends were sure the world would be poorer for his dying. When the majestic Figure on the central cross of Calvary gave up His life, His followers were sure that life forever would be immeasurably enriched by it. And it has been so. Somehow, folk of many creeds have been drawn to Him there, and have found assurance that in His death the black and terrible reality of sin received a fatal blow at its very roots.

The Cross, even more than the twisted cross, the swastika or the hammer and sickle, or the dollar sign, reveals sin's tremendous power; but it reveals also that which makes it a gospel: the power of perfect love and faith to take the worst that men can do, and transmute it into goodness. Love incarnate in a human personality identified itself so completely with us in our need and guilt that by personal commitment to that love we rise above the guilt and realize forgiveness. As the apostle Paul sang, half-breathless with the splendor of it, "God proves His love for us in that while we were yet sinners, Christ died for us."

No theology, no creedal system of man's devising, could effect the transforming results which this faith has produced. This deed, done in time on Golgotha's mount, must have been done in eternity within the heart of God. Apprehending something of the deep significance of Christ's sacrifice, and subdued to awe by His transcendent forgiveness of His enemies, we sometimes murmur, "God must be like that!" But as we glimpse the other, the eternal Calvary, we know that God *is that*; God is in Christ, reconciling the world to Himself. Through the clouds of Calvary there shines God's face. As an active volcano reveals the ageless fires burning in the earth's heart since the creation of the world, so the Action on Calvary reveals the eternal love of God our Father and our Redeemer.

Ever and always I can see, set up above this world of ours, a huge and towering cross with great arms stretched out East and West, from the rising to the setting sun, and on that cross my God still hangs and calls on all brave men and women to come out, and share His sorrow and help to save the world.[3]

> And even could I see Him die,
> I could but see a little part
> Of that great love which, like a fire,
> Is always burning in His heart.

Today, as in all the yesterdays, the Church of the living God bids men to trust this heroic and holy love; to make the choice which is the commitment to One who is our Saviour because He is the Love which endureth, believeth and hopeth all things for us.

> O dearly, dearly has He loved,
> And we must love Him too,
> And trust in His redeeming blood,
> And try His works to do.

Behold the two Calvaries, and make this childlike but adequate faith your own!

I saw two Calvaries, even while I reflected upon these things: one in the darkness of that first Good Friday, and the other in the light of Easter morn. When the pitifully small company of those who loved Him stood by the cross and heard Him utter the words, "It is finished!" do you not think that they felt the darkness enveloping life was utterly complete? So much that was lovely seemed finished forever. It was the blackout of every flickering hope. Jesus foresaw it on the eve of His death: "This is your hour, and the power of darkness."[4] What an interminable hour! It seems to have lasted until this moment, and despite brighter promise of military victory for our cause, the darkness spreads and deepens.

"It is finished," the darkness covers the earth. In one glorious sense nothing Christ did on Calvary was ended. His influence expands. His truth remains, and wings its way across every trench and boundary. Rome was not finished with Him, nor Jerusalem, nor our modern cities of dreadful night and glorious promise in this year of our Lord.

Look at Calvary in the glow of the first day of the week following the crucifixion. Irradiated now by a light which shines from beyond the ramparts of the world, it proclaims the Victory of God. Does that despairing cynic "inside" protest that this is the comforting illusion of religious faith, refuted by the grim facts of this year of strife? I know; there are the vast territories controlled by brutal men; the concentration camps; the myriads of nameless graves; the despoiled children and the starving nations. But look at the Cross from the vantage point of Olivet's shattered tomb. Nothing is finished until truth and justice, goodness and love, have their perfect way. Hatred, fear, cruelty and falsehood will never finish anything. He who made the Cross of shame a symbol of glory will complete the task God places in our hearts and hands. He shall see of the travail of His soul and be satisfied.

Ogden Nash may not be considered as useful homiletically as he is as a humorist, but in his volume of collected verse, *Good Intentions,* he has a striking poem in which he contrasts the Holy Night of long ago with the unholy horrors of total war. His conclusion strikes the authentic Christian note and expresses the conviction formed at Calvary:

> Gentlemen of the High Command,
> Who crucify the slums,
> There was an earlier Golgotha;
> The Third day comes.[5]

Aye, mark that, you tyrants who would enslave your brothers. Mark that too, ye who faint beneath the load of today's anguish: *the third day comes.*

As God lives and school children read, it comes. The Spirit that suffers with us in our sinning and in our sorrows, must reign. Why are we so sure? Because, as the New Testament declares: "He disarmed the principalities and powers and made a public example of them, triumphing over them in His Cross."[6] To Him who loves us and has freed us from our sins by His blood and has made us a Kingdom, priests to His God and Father, to Him be glory and dominion for ever and ever. Amen.

PRAYER: *Holy and loving Father whose blessed Son Jesus Christ as on this day didst enter the city where He was to die, enter Thou into our lives, cleansing our hearts of all that crucifies the Son of God afresh, clarifying our vision that we may discern Thy suffering with Thy children and Thy triumph over evil, reinforcing our wills to follow our Saviour in His patience and humility. So equip us with resources of Thy Spirit that taking up our Cross and entering into the fellowship of His sufferings, we may come at last to dwell with Him in His eternal Kingdom; through the same Jesus Christ our Lord. Amen.*

13

"Only the Truth Remains"

It is finished.   JOHN 19:30

> Friend, it is over now,
> The passion, the sweat, the pains,
> Only the truth remains.[1]

THUS speaks the Madman in John Masefield's play, *Good Friday*. Thus also may have spoken the heartbroken Mother and desolate friends of the Victim whose sufferings and death we commemorate. Three hours have passed since He cried, "It is finished!" "Father, into Thy hands I commend My Spirit." "He did not suffer long," said the sympathetic; "scarcely three hours." "It is finished," said John, "and I loved Him so." "It is finished," moaned the Mother, as she tried to lay her dreams for her Boy away. "Such an ending, when the stars sang together the night He came. It is cold and dark now. Take me home, John." "Well, it is over now," said Authority; "that menace to the established order is ended. Caesar should be grateful, and those wily churchmen, too."

> Friend, it is over now,
> The passion, the sweat, the pains . . .

Two tender-hearted men, now avowed disciples of the Crucified, came forward to ask for the body. Roman administration deferred to the varied religious sentiments of the people under their sway, and permission was granted for burial. A nearby rock-hewn tomb provided sepulcher. Love and reverence united to render the last tribute. The circular stone for closing the mouth of the tomb

112

was rolled across it, and Jesus of Nazareth was buried, "in a new tomb . . . in a garden."

"It is over now." "Finished." And yet, here are you and I, nineteen hundred years and a hemisphere distant from that event, under the spell of the tragedy and many of us glorying in it, too. It is *Good* Friday that we keep. For nineteen centuries of Christian experience attest that while the physical agonies and Palestine pilgrimage of Christ were ended as on this day outside a city wall, some things were ended by that Dying which exalt rather than depress our hearts.

When Jesus uttered the words, "It is finished!" He did so as a ship's commander might utter them to his first officer as a perilous voyage through dark and menacing seas ended in a friendly harbor. One glad exultant word in His native tongue sprang to His lips: "Finished!" "Accomplished!" His life perfected, His mission was fulfilled. History confirms the verdict. "He will never be surpassed," said Renan. "Higher has human thought not reached," mused Carlyle. Before the perfection of His personality it is absurd to speak of still fuller perfection. When a perfect chord in music is played, do we expect to hear a more perfect chord? Is not Christ, to use Robert Browning's phrase, "the C Major of this life"?[2] On the Cross, His character, His life, His disclosure of God were perfected, brought to a successful issue. Our fathers dwelt lovingly on this thought. They spoke frequently of the "finished work of the Redeemer." Is there not timeless truth in the old phrase? All through His life beneath the Syrian blue, He had sought to make God's nature known, His help available, His Kingdom actual. Yet one final act must be done to complete it. He must offer Himself, utterly, completely. He was sure that we could never escape the meaning and the power of that. On the Cross the supreme offering of Love was made. How our speech limps as we seek to express to ourselves all that was finished there. Something was done on Calvary that could never be done by any other. Something was done there that need never be done again. He—this Victim who is the Victor—

blazed a trail into the innermost depths of Reality. He opened a
new and living way into the Holiest of all. That trail once marked
remains for all time. Forever, all who would attain oneness
with the God and Father of Jesus Christ must come by this path.
He could do no more. "When He had overcome the sharpness of
death He opened the Kingdom of Heaven to all believers."

Do you remember hearing of the Royal Corps of Signallers'
picture? Painted for the Corps after World War I, the artist
depicted an incident which had occurred under shell fire. A
signaller is shown lying lifeless. He had been commissioned to
repair a cable snapped by enemy guns. The picture shows him
dead in the fulfillment of his task, holding together in his stiffen-
ing hands the broken ends of the wire. Contact had been re-
established. Beneath the painting was the one word, "Through!"
No wonder, as Hubert L. Simpson observed,[3] that Christians have
gazed at this picture of the crucifixion painted by the artists
whom we call the Evangelists, and felt that the same word might
be inscribed below. "Through" the willful perverseness and
blind stupidity of man to the justice and mercy of God; "through"
the darkness of defeat and death to the victory of life immortal;
"through" our Lord Jesus Christ.

> Friend, it is over now,
> The passion, the sweat, the pains,
> Only the truth remains.

This truth which the Cross burns into the consciousness of all
who ponder it, also affirms that in one profound sense nothing
was finished there. Life is pitifully brief at best. How rarely we
may say of someone vanished into the Unseen, "Well, he finished his work." Charles Dickens finished much, but *The Mystery
of Edwin Drood* was left but partly written. Livingstone never
lived to see the open sore of the African slave trade completely
healed. Many more than Cecil Rhodes could cry at the end, "So
little done, so much to do!" And in a world of war, these young
crusaders who throng up the old road to paradise in loyalty to a

thing not seen with the eyes—who can say that such lives are finished here? The unfinished symphonies in human hearts compel us to believe in further opportunities beyond this fugitive and fragmentary existence we call human life.

So with the Man on the Cross, but more deeply than of any other. "In one sense nothing He did was ended." His words could not sink into oblivion. His influence could not be confined to a forgotten grave on which Syrian stars look down. His truth remains. When He was interred it was only that His truth might wing its way across the earth and down the years. Rome was not finished with Him, nor Jerusalem, nor our modern cities of dreadful night and splendid promise in this year of our Lord.

Remember this, all ye who pass by with downcast eyes and discouraged minds! Truth may be nailed to a cross and taken down; sealed within a tomb. But truth rises again! "Though all the winds of doctrine were let loose to play upon the earth, so Truth be in the field, we do injuriously to misdoubt her strength. Let her and Falsehood grapple. Whoever knew Truth put to the worse in a free and open encounter?" Yes, I know; John Milton could never have foreseen the time when truth might not have a free and open encounter. Concentration camps, trampled minorities, despoiled little countries—Poland, Finland, Czechoslovakia and the rest—could not have occurred to him. But Christ said, "I am the Truth." Not all the truth, but the Truth which makes other truths indestructible. And He lives. Good Friday passes,

> Easter Day breaks!
> Christ rises! Mercy every way is infinite. . . .[4]

You see, the Cross was not a terminal, but a point of departure. No more vital personality moves among the stricken souls of earth than the Living Lord. Today, as in all the yesterdays since the first Good Friday, He makes the Father of all men known, and He brings the Father near in forgiving love and moral reinforcement. He must reign, whose right it is to reign.

Look you on that Cross and upon Him who triumphed over it,

transforming a device of shame into a symbol of victory. Look upon Him who is the pledge of truth's ultimate conquest, and love's final success. Let Good Friday see your feet and mine once more on His royal way, that we too may help to make up that which is lacking in Christ's sufferings. Nothing is finished until goodness and love have their perfect way. Hatred, fear, cruelty, falsehood will never finish anything. But the spirit of Him who died upon the Cross and lives forever will complete the task God places in our hearts and hands. What our Lord finished remains our unfinished task. The battle is joined now, and the result is sure. He shall see of the travail of His soul and be satisfied.

> Friend, it is over now,
> The passion, the sweat, the pains,
> Only the truth remains.

And the truth remains to be lived.

PRAYER: *Enable us, O Lord, to glory in Thy finished work; and grant that we may be able to finish what Thou hast granted us the wish to begin; through Jesus Christ our Redeemer. Amen.*

14
Present—Tense; Future—Perfect

By now they were approaching the village to which they were going; and He made as if He was going still farther. But they pressed Him, saying, "Stay with us, for it is near evening and there's not much daylight left."

LUKE 24:28, 29 (Manson)

Two men are driving along a prairie road to town. They "take it easy"; ditches with gumbo wait to grab their wheels. They have talked about many things as neighbors will; how the stock weathered the winter, when seeding might begin, how Jennie and the wee one are making out, taxes, and the like. Taxes and politics bring their words to the war in Korea and what Joe may be conniving in Moscow; what it will do to us over here. Nodding their heads vigorously, you hear them agreeing about one fact: things are bad. And what's around the corner is likely to be grim, really rugged—no mistake.

"It's tough any way you look at it, Bill. Take that boy of mine, he's never lived in a world without war brewing or breaking out. Even if there is a truce in Korea, another war is likely to break out any day. And we'll all be in it. I guess it's like what a fellow on the radio said the other night: we're going to live in a kind of garrison state from now on." "It is tough, Mac," agrees his friend, as they both bounce over a culvert. "Five years ago I really thought that United Nations outfit would be the answer, that it would help to settle things without fighting and killing. But now—the U. N. doesn't seem to be so much, gives the Commies a chance to lambaste the rest of us. Wouldn't you think the U. N. would have saved us from another mess, kept us from blowing each other to pieces?"

117

Two men trekking along a battered Korean trail somewhere near the thirty-eighth parallel. "Brother," one mutters to the other, "I would like to know the score. Here we are thousands of miles from home, serving under the U. N. flag. On V-J Day, six years ago, I was one who thought that our government along with the others in the U. N. would have solved the problem without an 'operation killer.' " To which his companion adds his agreement: "You're right . . . What's the matter with people, not just the Russians and Mao's men but us, and our kind? Have we been fooling ourselves that we could have a world where folks of different countries and ideas could live together like human beings?"

Two men—or were they man and wife?—walk along a country road to the village where they lived. "What kind of a world is this?" asks one. "Isn't there anything we can count on in religion? Here was this Man, and somehow I still think He was more than a man—God-man, Peter called Him. If anyone could have saved us and our people without lifting a spear, it was this Jesus. I had hoped that He would have been the One . . . but now He's finished like a common criminal, on a cross . . . it makes a person wonder if God cares . . ."

Men like ourselves moving along roads in Canada, in America, in Asia, in Palestine . . . Trying to face the facts, deserving full marks for living with dark reality. How would you describe their outlook—theirs and ours? Here is one phrase that comes from those lessons in grammar we had back in school, used then for words, usable now for our inner mood and outward prospect:

"Present—*tense*; future . . ."

Well, what is the future? No doubt about the first; any candid camera shot of our condition would show tensions—between power groups in the world community, and in us. What about the future? Would it be just plain sense to say the future will be black, dreadful, something that will not bear thinking about?

"Present—*tense*; future—*blank*"—unless there is another factor operating; a power and a purpose with goodness and justice at the heart of it.

That is just what there is at the heart of this difficult and dangerous enterprise we call living. This is the Good News, the wonder, the truth of Easter. For the Gospel for this Easter night and every night and day points to the infinite factor in our human situation. What do those wizards with numbers, the mathematicians, say?—multiply infinity with any factor, and the result is infinity. What does the living Word of God say? In substance this: multiply divinity—the God and Father of our Lord Jesus Christ—with any factor, and the result will be divine.

Now listen again to part of the report on the two discouraged travelers trudging to their village on the first Easter evening. The two have been joined by a Third who is the key to the problem that perplexes them. "By now they were approaching the village to which they were going; and He made as if He was going still farther. But they pressed Him saying, 'Stay with us, for it is near evening and there's not much daylight left.' So—He—went—in—to stay with them." Divine Love reached down into the human scene giving men the clue to the grand drama of life.

If Easter means that death and evil could not defeat or hold Christ, then it means *that* for us, if we are linked to Him. It means that for all who trust and serve the Love and Wisdom and Power that is God, it is a case of present—tense . . . future—perfect. You see, the disclosure, the revelation of Easter is that God has the last word, and that word is life, peace, joy, victory. The present is tense, and in this kind of world the Christian cannot escape tension. The pull between two kinds of power—the power of evil and the strange power men call weakness, holy, righteous Love—that kind of tension is likely to continue. True, if you commit yourself to God in Christ, commit all that you know of yourself to all that you know of God in Him, you will know release from many inner tensions. But while there will be peace at the center, you will encounter war around you.

Do you say, "Then isn't this rather stupid optimism to speak in the same breath of the future being perfect?" Is it? If by perfect you mean the end of striving, the end of tears, the end of sacrifice in this mortal stretch of our existence, then perfection is not promised. But if being made perfect is what matters; if growth toward maturity in our relationships with others and toward God; if inward reinforcement for every need is part of going on toward perfection—then it is true: present—tense; future—perfect.

Does this mean that living by the faith of the Son of God who loved us and gave Himself for us and has been raised from the dead by the power of God, we shall be free from pain and loss? No; the Cross remains the symbol of this faith. But it does mean that the cloud over Hiroshima need not cast its shadow over all the years ahead. For it means that when we move along the road of God's will for His human family He Himself draws near . . . that when our dark hours come, as come they do, the miracle of Easter in Emmaus is repeated: He comes in to stay with us, and then leads us farther. And coming He brings meaning, and with the meaning, peace, and in the peace, power to do what His spirit commands. The fact of the Risen Lord enabled St. Paul to say, "I consider that the sufferings of this present time are not worth comparing with the glory that is to be revealed to us."

> There is no dark despair that cannot be
> Evicted from the heart's Gethsemane;
> For faith is always more than unbelief,
> And vibrant courage triumphs over grief.[1]

Easter attests this incontrovertible fact: God vindicated the most perfect life, even the life of the Son of His love. Lift up your hearts. Yes, lift them up unto the Lord. For He must reign, until all His enemies are put under His feet. Present—tense, at least anxious? But the present belongs to Him, and the future is in His hands. Receive His gift of eternal life—knowledge of God through trust in Him and Jesus Christ whom He has sent. Then you and I and all our brothers in the faith can conquer the forces of the present that bring death to men's souls—war, racial hatreds, lies and deceits, injustice.

What about the long future? After all, even if we can and must learn to handle the split atom and the menace of predatory communism, there is the last Enemy. But Christ is Risen; He has put down the last enemy, Death. There are no permanent bereavements. Physical death remains, but no death can touch the real *you*, if, as Paul would say, you are "in Christ," united to Him in loving trust and obedience. In the January, 1951, issue of *Atlantic* magazine, Donald C. Babcock had an unusual poem he called "Pre-Valedictory." It is full of the Resurrection faith concerning your own personal future—after you are born out of the body:

> . . . by the Eternal, I am not expendable.
> No, do not speculate on where I have gone.
> The guides on this journey do not speak our language.
> I have long contemplated reduction to my essential being.
> Now regard me as having slipped into the finer interstices
>   of the universe of Spirit.
> Take heed to St. Paul, and do not ask
> "With what manner of body . . . ?"
> *Why, I wouldn't be caught dead with a body.*
>
> Should you care to note my withdrawal
> In the manner that best links spirit and matter,
> Play the Emperor Concerto, second movement, and disperse
> But cheerfully.[2]

The more we live in our love and active immortality, the more greatly we live, most of all as we live in Christ. One of my German colleagues told me that during the last weeks of World War I, two characteristic communiqués were issued, one by the German high command, and the other by Austrian headquarters. The first read: "The situation is serious, but not hopeless." The next day the Austrian headquarters issued a statement saying: "The situation is hopeless, but not serious." For the Christian fighter it is like that: "Situation now—hopeless; but not serious, not irreparable, not final." Why? Because even when it seems as if "there's not much daylight left," the Light of the world draws near. He makes Himself known supremely within His community: the Church. May I inject this personal word? For nearly two years I have had opportunity to observe the churches of North America as I could not when I was a parish minister. Of course I am not an unprejudiced witness—how could I be who owe so much to Christ and His Church? But I am convinced more than ever that the Church in all its branches is the light and salt of society, the custodian and transmitter of the truth that can set us free from error, impotence and despair. Despite the frailty and follies of her members, she is the Community of the Resurrection, the living Body of Christ. Support her, not at Easter only, but every week.

> Souls of the years to come,
> Christ guide you on your way,
> Into this world, and out again.
> He knows the way to come and go—
> Comes with a star, goes with a cross,
> And comes again with a triumph;
> He is risen.[3]

This is the fact, the claim, the promise and the truth this Eastertide: "Present—tense; situation hopeless—from man's perspective; but not serious—for there is always Christ . . . future—*perfect*."

PRAYER: *Almighty and eternal God, who on Easter Day didst turn the despair of the disciples into triumph by the resurrection of Christ who had been crucified, give us now assurance of Thy victory over evil and death within us and within our world.*

O living Lord, whose touch makes all things new, make us sharers of Thy life, strong and free, glad and triumphant. Inspire in Thy people of America, of the world, energy of mind and spirit, that with courage and enthusiasm we may meet life eager and unafraid; in the power of Him who is more than conqueror in all things, Jesus Christ our Lord. Amen.

15
Why Did He Return?

And ye now therefore have sorrow: but I will see you again, and your heart shall rejoice, and your joy no man taketh from you.　JOHN 16:22

Then the same day at evening, being the first day of the week, when the doors were shut where the disciples were assembled for fear . . . came Jesus and stood in the midst, and saith unto them, Peace be unto you.　JOHN 20:19

ON THURSDAY night around the supper table the Master told His first disciples that after His death He would return to them. "Ye now therefore have sorrow: but I will see you again, and your heart shall rejoice."

On the following Sunday from early morning until night He revealed Himself alive. To the women who had gone to perform love's last tender rites for the dead, to Peter, to the two forlorn travelers to Emmaus, to the eleven depressed men huddling around the table in their rendezvous in the Upper Room, as later to many others, He kept His seemingly impossible promise. As Luke the physician recorded: "He had shown himself alive to them after He had suffered, in many convincing ways, appearing to them through forty days, and telling them about the Kingdom of God."[1]

This is what Easter is all about. In a profound sense, this is what the Christian religion is all about. Jesus of Nazareth, who taught and healed in Palestine, who made men sure of God, healed their physical and spiritual hurts, invited them to a daring and joyous adventure in living, involved Himself in their struggles and sorrows, and was put to death by Roman authorities, is alive now and forevermore. The Lord is present with His people. That Jesus Christ rose from the dead in a real and vital

123

way is the central conviction of the Christian. He did more than teach the resurrection. He Himself *was . . . is . . .* the resurrection, the visible embodiment of infinite vitality. "I will see you again," He said. "A little while, and ye shall not see Me: and again, a little while, and ye shall see Me. . . ." And in that "little while" He experienced death on a cross, "was crucified, dead, and buried" (as the old creed has it).

"Then the same day . . . being the first day of the week, when the doors were shut where the disciples were assembled for fear . . . came Jesus and stood in the midst, and saith unto them, Peace be unto you. . . . Then were the disciples glad when they saw the Lord."

If you ask us how it all happened, we must answer that we do not know. But that it did happen, nineteen centuries of Christian experience affirms.

An editor visiting the seaside once encountered an old fisherman along the cliffs near the sea. He was struck by the old man's simple faith in his Lord. "How do you know that Christ is risen and is in this world?" asked the newspaperman. "Sir," came the reply, "do you see those cottages near the cliffs? Well, sir, sometimes when I'm far out at sea, I know the sun is risen by the light that is reflected from yon windows. How do I know that Christ is risen? Why, sir, do I not see His light reflected from the faces of some of my fellow men every day, and do I not feel the light of His glory in my own life? As soon tell me that the sun is not risen when I see his reflected glory as tell me that my Lord is not risen!"

> No more in Galilee we look for Thee,
>   O Risen Lord;
> In every land and on each moonlit sea
>   Thy voice is heard;
> And when Thy saints are gathered in Thy Name,
>   Closer Thou art to each than fire to flame.[2]

Jesus Christ returned. To different eyes, and to different personalities He came in different ways. But He came. And He comes. He is "the same yesterday, today and forever."

Why did He come back? Sometimes we have spoken of the resurrection fact as if the Master returned to buttress the disciples' belief in immortality. Doubtless Christ's victory over death did that, does it still. But even a majority of His enemies assumed that after His execution Jesus would survive somewhere in some fashion. The reasons must lie deeper. Did He return to add some significant truth to His teaching? It does not seem likely. On the Cross He had cried, "It is finished!" In a profound sense His work, His ministry of teaching, was completed. After the resurrection, the Risen Lord did not propound any new doctrine, nor give an extra parable, nor add another petition to the Model Prayer. Nor did He impart any new information concerning heaven or hell.

Why did He return?

Let me put it as simply as I can: *Christ returned to comfort and to command His followers.*

How He comforted them! "Peace be unto you!" "Ought not the Christ to have suffered these things before entering into His glory?" "Lo, I am with you alway, even unto the end of the world."

How He commanded His friends! "Go ye, therefore, and make disciples of all nations. . . . As the Father hath sent Me, even so send I You. Ye shall be my witnesses both in Jerusalem . . . and to the uttermost parts of the earth. . . . Lovest thou Me? Feed My sheep!"

We need comfort. And He returned to give it. Comfort is a far stronger word than we commonly think. In current usage it is too often reduced to a soothing pat on a childlike head. But of course it means an infusion of strength, of fortitude. While we use it today to mean "console," originally it meant to support, to invigorate. It is in this more rugged sense that we need comfort today. He came back to invigorate dispirited men. They were sure the Cross wrote a lurid "finis" to the drama of the life of Lives. The props beneath them had all fallen when their Leader's lifeless body was laid in Joseph's tomb. Then He returned. Simon Peter, wallowing in self-disparagement became living granite. Thomas, embittered by his broken hopes, plunged into skepticism, became a triumphant, intrepid believer. Mary, sure that she had lost her Lord forever, was found by Him, and her sorrow was transmuted into lyrical joy. John, bereft of His dearest friend, rediscovered Him, inseparable, imperishable. Men and women who were defeated became victors. A little, pitiful, broken company was transformed into the holy catholic Church!

He returned to comfort them with the assurance that at the heart of what seemed a terrifying cosmic indifference the living and loving God reigns. This universe is friendly to the noblest hopes of man. This spinning planet is guided and guarded by an eternal Love. Jesus Christ could not be held captive by the forces of evil and death.

Is not this immense, immeasurable comfort? That this vast process, of which we are tiny but meaningful parts, is not going it blind, but fulfilling the design of its mighty and wise Architect? That lives committed to the loving purpose of the Christlike Father are not at the mercy of chance, of wind and weather? That Christlike causes dedicated to the liberation and enhancement of human personalities, though crucified shall rise again? That in the darkest hour we can look up and say "Our Father," and know our cry is heard, and understood; hear Him say, "My child. . . ."?

He knew, too, that we would need the comfort of a great assurance concerning our loved ones who have vanished from our side. Love does not willingly believe in the extinction of its object. No one can say, God so loved us that He sent His Son in order that believing in Him we might love Him in return, for a few years before we suffer complete extinction. So He returned that we might know that love never faileth, even before the assaults of death. Because He lives, we know that all who live in Him live eternally. Trust in the Risen Lord enabled a bereaved soul to inscribe on the tombstone of his beloved in a south of England graveyard: "Gone home with a friend."

We need this comfort. You and I need to know that life, in

spite of all its inexplicable disasters and tragedies, has splendid meaning, unlimited possibilities, ever-expanding horizons. Christ returned to write beneath His own interpretation: "Proven" . . . Q.E.D. He returns still to exercise this divine ministry of information and inspiration. Not now in bodily form, but in spirit and in truth He comes to those who keep in His fellowship, who maintain honest quest of truth, and who welcome Him. You— I—can know His blessed presence, on any road, in any place. Within you can glow the fire divine burning, even now—to borrow John Wesley's words—"with inextinguishable blaze"!

> No distant Lord have I,
>   Loving afar to be.
> Made flesh for me He cannot rest
>   Until He rests in me.
>
> I need not journey far
>   This dearest friend to see.
> Companionship is always mine;
>   He makes His home with me.
>
> I envy not the twelve,
>   Nearer to me is He.
> The life He once lived here on earth
>   He lives again in me.[3]

"I will see you again," He said. "A little while, and ye shall see Me." "When the doors were shut . . . for fear . . . came Jesus and stood in the midst, and saith unto them, Peace be unto you."

He came not only to comfort, but to command. The first Easter brought not only the assurance timid and desponding hearts required; it brought the directive which gave world-transforming purpose. To the promise of His empowering presence He attached a condition: "Go . . . and, lo, I am with you. . . ." We must do His will if we would have His presence. Still He comes as of old. He asks, "Lovest thou Me?" "Yea, Lord, thou knowest. . . ." "Then feed my sheep." What does that mean, Master? Food is still needed, and clothing, and such economic help that will enable war-impoverished communities to help themselves . . . He turns to the teacher, to the preacher, to the church member: "Lovest thou Me?" "Yea, Lord." Tend my sheep. Feed my sheep. They must be taught the basic truths of revealed religion . . . That girl who is lonely needs food of friendship. That business-man whose morale is slipping even more than his halo . . . That boy struggling for an education, fighting sometimes wildly to sort out his standards . . . That bewildered, love-starved child from a broken home, or one that is completely secularized: "Feed My sheep. Feed My lambs."

Get yourself out of the way; get in there and help. Forget about your place, your security, your power. Men and women around the earth are famished for lack of nourishment for bodies, minds and spirits. You want to know about communism versus capitalism; totalitarianism versus freedom? "Follow thou me. . . ."

He commands: "Go! Bear witness! Feed my sheep! Tend my lambs! Win the nations to the standard of the Cross."

> And none of them durst ask Him, Who art thou? knowing that it was the Lord. And He said unto them, "As the Father hath sent Me into the world, even so send I you." And He blessed them there; and the room where they worked, the place where they served, the Church or chapel where they wor-shipped—was luminous with His presence.[5]

Do you say, "Wouldn't it be wonderful if this could happen now?" But it can. Thomas Carlyle gave a valuable hint. He said the supreme requirement for knowing a great figure in thought, literature or life is what he called "lovingness." That is a primary requisite for knowing the risen Christ. "We have, with the early disciples," wrote McEwan Lawson, "to go home with Him, to stand in the room where His Spirit dwells, and with humble 'lovingness' to learn of Him." Keep in the fellowship; for it is a sacrament of Christ's self-giving.

Above all, remember He is alive in His world now. You never know when and where you will encounter Him. Someone asked, Who is this man Plato? And the answer was immediate: Plato is the man whom we always meet coming back on whatsoever avenue of truth we enter. Who is this Master, Jesus? One answer surely is this: Jesus Christ is the Risen and Victorious Lord whom we always meet on whatsoever avenue of loving service and obedient faith we tread.

Why did He return? Because He and you were made for each other! Because we must have God; and somehow, God must have us! This is why He returned: to comfort and command you and me.

PRAYER: *O Risen and Victorious Christ, ever-living and ever-present, abide Thou in us: may we abide in Thee. That we may see the Father as Thou seest Him, that we may bring forth fruit, utterly self-forgetful; that Thy love for all men may burn within our hearts, that the Father's will may be done in the world through us; that Love alone may live in us, and that we may live by the power of an endless life. Lord, we abide in Thee: abide Thou in us. Amen.*

16

"Can These Bones Live?"

Can these bones live? And I answered, O Lord God, thou knowest. Then he said to me, Prophesy . . . So I prophesied as he commanded me, and the breath came into them, and they lived, and stood upon their feet, an exceeding great army.   EZEKIEL 37:3, 4; 10

Can world order be achieved? Is our present civilization fated to follow its twenty predecessors into oblivion? Can decent, high-minded individuals be drawn together into a "fellowship of the concerned"? Is there any chance of Christians of diverse types becoming a mighty army, united in Him whom all acknowledge as Lord and Leader?

These are big questions, crucial and urgent. For time runs on and out. What answer shall we give? Much more important, what answer does the Lord of history give?

If we face such questions at all, most of us answer in one of two ways. Either we yield to despair concerning mankind's plight; or, we whistle up our courage, assume a brave optimism which is not a little shaky at its roots, and say, "We'll make out all right." It is here that vital religion goes deeper than bland optimism or secular despair. With pitiless honesty, Christian faith uncovers the dire plight into which we have drifted, and at the same time reveals the infinite factor in human affairs which makes all the difference.

Here is what I mean. Rather, here is what prophetic religion means. It is stated in terms of a strange picture drawn about five centuries before Christ. A Jewish exile saw his nation die. He refused to take that death as death. "The NO of the present he met with an Everlasting YEA. For he believed God." This man,

Ezekiel, had a dream. In it he sees a valley of dried bones. Whose bleached bones litter this desolate glen? His fellow exiles. Like the vast disarray of bleached skeletons strewn before him, his fellow countrymen are scattered, confused, lifeless. Their doom is complete. "And, lo, they were very dry. And the Lord said unto me, Son of Man, can these bones live?" And I answered, O Lord God, thou knowest." (It was Ezekiel's way of avoiding the only answer he could give—"No." There was no earthly reason why those bones should live.) "And he said unto me, Prophesy over these bones, and say to them, O ye dry bones, hear the word of the Lord. Thus saith the Lord God to these bones, Behold! I am causing breath to enter you, and you shall live." The prophet spoke as he was commanded, and in that eerie Death Valley he heard a rustling: "And the bones came together, bone to its bone. And as I looked, lo! there were sinews upon them, and flesh came up, and skin covered them over; but there was no breath in them."

Talk about a vivid and splendid passage, with modern parallels! We have organized the good life; drawn our blueprints and forged the machinery for peace, outlined a better life for the people, and provided as adequate a framework for the spiritual life as we know how to devise. And whatever shrill advocates of scrapping all the machinery say, or dreamy-eyed mystics urge in the name of simplicity, we do not propose to scrap it all. Organization *is* necessary. Mere diffused good will cannot save us. Disembodied ideas, even when nobly conceived and conferred, make feeble ghosts. To extricate ourselves from chaos, we need organization. To create peace we must fashion a system, with wheels within wheels. As for the spiritual life, we never can transmit the good news about God in Christ without a transmitter. Destroy the Church today and tomorrow we would be compelled to create another. But structures, systems, organizations of themselves are not enough. Forms without force are like an elaborate chain of cables and wires strung across the country, unconnected to any power station. The skeleton of organization may be complete, may be clothed with the sinews and flesh of required forms, and yet be lifeless.

"But there was no breath in them," observed Ezekiel.

Worried man stands on the street corner, looks at the building housing the peacemakers; glances at the churches, chapels and other temples of faith; ponders the lighted halls of Congress and Parliament, and says something as hopeless and final, "They are dead. There's no life in them."

But God has another word. He is the God not of the dead, but of the living, said One who came much later than Ezekiel and of whom friends said, "In Him was life." The God with whom Ezekiel was in close contact bade him prophesy again, impelled him to deliver this empowering message: "Thus says the Lord God: Come from the four winds, O breath, and breathe into these slain men, that they may live! So I prophesied as He commanded me, and the breath came into them, and they lived, and stood upon their feet, an exceeding great army." It is clear what the vision meant to Ezekiel. He told us quite plainly. The bones in that Valley of his vision were the whole house of Israel. The breath was the Spirit of God. The incident is the dream of a displaced person who was in direct, intimate touch with the living God. Despite the fall of his nation, the ruin of so much which seemed irreplaceable, he believes that God is able and will restore the nation. The dream is a prediction of the national resurrection under the mighty hand of God. It is matter of history that the resuscitation took place after many years. God brought the exiles home. He revitalized the moribund community.

If it could only happen here! If it could only happen now in this distracted and despairing world!

In the Lord's name I say unto you that *it can happen here and now*: that in plain fact it is happening in one area after another as our keenest observers testify; that it can happen in our beloved land, in the community where we live and work.

You have a right to know the reasons for such confidence.

First and foremost and all the time, there is *the fact of the Holy*

Spirit. Do you feel that this is the most mysterious part of the Faith? Perhaps you could answer quite honestly in the words of the dozen men Paul found at Ephesus. When he asked them about the divine Spirit, they replied, "We have not so much as heard whether there be any Holy Ghost." They knew about Jesus, His Cross and resurrection, but they did not know that He had returned in the coming of the Spirit at Pentecost. But when Jesus passed from sight, no one who knew anything about Him or His love could imagine that He would pass out of our lives. He had given His word, that He would be with His followers "alway, even unto the end of the world." That promise was literally fulfilled. That is the doctrine of the Holy Spirit. He promised that He would return; He used the sign every Jew knew and liked: He breathed upon the dispirited disciples in their hideaway in Jerusalem, and said, "Receive ye the Holy Spirit." Remember that after the resurrection many Christians had never seen Jesus on earth. But they were sure that He was with them, that He influenced their lives profoundly, that they had His Spirit. He had been "prisoner of an hour and place"; now He was unfettered by time or space. When they yielded to His Spirit they had power unlimited; not just their own energies released but an access of supernatural power.

Of course Judaism knew of the Spirit. The second verse of the Bible speaks of the Spirit of God hovering over the face of the waters. From earliest times men noticed and tried to account for the extraordinary achievements of ordinary men and women. They were sure that the mysterious power was God's action. As they developed in understanding they came to see that the Spirit must be a power making for goodness in the lives of men and entire communities. Thus Ezekiel describes God breathing His breath or Spirit into the dried bones. For Christians it is the distinctive doctrine. Jesus Himself, we say, returned to His Church as the Holy Spirit. Today is the anniversary of that spiritual return, the birthday of the Church. Pentecost means that God Himself caused the dead bones of His Church to be clothed with the sinews of faith and the flesh of vital fellowship to confront the vast host of paganism "an exceeding great army."

A little girl having tea with her friend in an apartment was startled to hear music and conversation from the people next door. Her young hostess announced triumphantly, "In our house we have neighbors just through the wall." Jesus taught something like that about God. God is our near neighbor, but He lives not just beyond the wall. He comes to our own door. As the Master might have knocked at the door of a fisherman's cottage in Galilee, so His Spirit seeks entrance into our lives. "Behold, I stand at the door" to bring life, joy, peace and power.

This is the living Gospel, the demonstration of the Spirit and of power, from Pentecost to the last redeemed waif of a city's slum or a suburb's privileged neighborhood. Without this Gospel, even the teaching of Jesus is only a teaching of the past.

A recent British visitor to America, Dr. Alec Vidler, wrote that the pattern of North American preaching is, "Let me suggest that you try to be good." Whatever that is, it is not apostolic preaching! Nor is it likely to produce apostolic success. Over against it set Peter's blunt demand, "Repent, and be baptized every one of you in the name of the Lord Jesus Christ, for the forgiveness of your sins; and you shall receive the gift of the Holy Spirit."[1] See yourselves as you really are, says the apostle. Join the poor in Spirit, and you will be blessed. You will not need to pray for the Spirit; you will have it, or rather, you will have Him.

Was there ever a time when more people wanted to be good, or wanted more earnestly a good world in which peace and health and comradely living would prevail? And the world was never nearer catastrophe! When men try to be good by their own unaided wills they produce instruments of annihilation. Who was it that suggested the preamble to the American Constitution be amended to read, "We hold this truth to be self-evident, that all men shall be *cremated* equal"? Instead of trying to be good, we might try in repentance and faith to receive the power of God.

"Can these dry bones live?" Indeed they can, as the Spirit of God has access to them, to us.

The divine action is evident. For the fruits of the Spirit, transformed lives in a divinely energized community, are the evidence.

This leads me to cite a further reason for our sublime confidence that lifeless souls and communities can be vitalized by divine power, the power of Christlike love and wisdom. It is this: *the miracle is being worked by God Himself.* Individuals are being transformed. Here at home men and women are tapping reservoirs of spiritual power, are finding energy to become unified, whole and wholesome personalities. Emotional life is being cleansed and steadied; hearts are being mended, control of appetites is being restored, homes are being pulled together. It is more than vitamins, psychoanalysis, or some deep-breathing exercises that is the secret! The action may be as the fire, purging, purifying, tempering the steel; it may be as

> . . . that gentle voice we hear,
>   Soft as the breath of even,
> That checks each fault, that calms each fear,
>   And speaks of heaven

not only after physical death but here and now. Whatever the mode of operation, uncounted men and women know that

> . . . every virtue we possess,
>   And every victory won,
> And every thought of holiness
>   Are His alone.[2]

As for the evidence in the newer Christian communities, overseas in Africa and Asia, it is sheer romance, the romance of the Spirit of God.

Does it not thrill you, to recall that the last one hundred and fifty years have been the years of fiercest battle that the Christian Church had to wage? That during this same period the Cross of Christ has won more triumphs than in any other era since the first age of Christianity? So much so, says one cautious student of the movement, that if Christianity were to die out in Europe and America, it would live in Asia, would be established in Africa and in the islands of the southern seas. "The tranquil operation of God's perpetual Providence is carrying out man's redemption." The power of the Holy Spirit is flooding the power of God into the life of the world in ways which make us exclaim, "This is the Lord's doing, and it is marvellous in our eyes!"

And what will you make of that which Archbishop Temple called the "great new fact of our time"—the emergence of the world-wide Christian fellowship, the ecumenical movement? In spite of deadly conservatism, deadening prejudice, the branches— the bones—of the Christian denominations are drawing together. Christians are weary of the "cult of the incomplete"—sectarianism. The churches are rediscovering their unity, are determined by God's grace to present a united front to the sorely divided world; are coming through the fires of adversity, themselves fired by zeal to realize their oneness in Christ and recapture the lost provinces of the Kingdom of God for Him. The calendar of the twentieth century will have one entry which may become historic, prophetic and another Pentecost. It is the date AMSTERDAM, 1948. In that Netherlands city, during August of that year, representatives of over 130 churches met to pray, to plan, to create the first World Council of the Church since the far-off age when the Church was outwardly undivided although actually confined to Europe and the Near East. It may well be appraised one hundred years hence as the most significant event of the twentieth century.

"Can these bones live?" You have wondered, and frankly you have written off these slow-moving, reactionary and divided institutions of the ideal. You see the Church as every lover of truth has seen it, a valley of dry bones. But listen: do you not hear the rustling of the Spirit? Do you not see this apparently lifeless mass becoming again the Fellowship of the Concerned? Lift up your heart! These bones shall live.

Lift up thy head and hark what sounds are in the dark,
For His feet are coming to thee on the waters![3]

"There was a sound; and lo! there followed a rustling . . . and they lived and stood upon their feet—an exceeding great army." I believe in the holy catholic Church, the Communion of Saints, because I believe in the Holy Ghost, the Lord and Giver of Life.

"Can these bones live?" Can the skeleton organization of peace, of community betterment, of your own church, become radiantly, creatively alive again; become a living, invincible legion of brave sacrificial hearts? *It depends on you—and God.*

Have you been occupying the cynic's seat, the box reserved for the scornful? Get down in the arena where brave and generous souls struggle on. Have you joined in the lampooning and disparagement of church groups? God knows the average is low enough in intellectual acumen and even in simple kindliness, so often are we absorbed in pitiful trivialities. Always the cure of such conditions is more of the Spirit of Christ. Get in there—not to fight or carp or merely diagnose and prescribe! Get in there and help. Take your part again in your own local congregation to make the Church what you know it ought to become, can become, too, since Christ loved it and gave His life for it. At the end of the day, God will not ask you what kind of a church you belonged to, but what kind of a church you longed for. Longed for enough—that is—to pray for, witness within, and strive for. Remember always that the resuscitation of any moribund household depends upon its members becoming disciplined, trained, united in the things that matter. This means that we must place ourselves at the disposal of the Spirit of God who is at once the interpreter of the truth, the companion of our spirits, and the empowerment for serving Christlike ends. It simply will not do to be one of "a mere crowd of good people milling about the world." The Christian enterprise is not a picnic. The living Church of Jesus Christ is no mere collection of good people who believe in being and doing good after their fashion. It is an ex-

ceeding great army of skilful and disciplined, men and women.
As Dr. L. P. Jacks of Oxford once remarked, "it is not a standing
army either, but a marching one, always on the move, always
advancing with a united front, with perfect order as the key of
advance."

I would speak a more intimate word to the comrades of the
Way discouraged by their slow personal progress. You sigh,
"Where is the blessedness I knew, when first I saw the Lord?"
You would give anything to recover spiritual vitality. Living
seems so lusterless that you are tempted to say, "Our bones are
dried up, our hope is lost; we are clean cut off." You have tried.
God in His love knows how you have tried. What if now you
should stop striving? Let God work His miracle in you and
through you. In the Valley of Dried Bones the bones did not
clothe, reanimate, marshal themselves. The Spirit of God worked
the miracle. He will work it again. Only you must place yourself
in line with His will. You must keep close to the spiritual Christ.
It was a sad day in the life of a little Italian lad when his favorite
artist died. He went to the house, asked the widow for one of the
great man's brushes. Wistfully he said, "I think I could paint
like the great master if only I had one of his brushes." She smiled
understandingly, took him to the studio, and granted his request.
Eagerly the boy dipped the brush into the colors and began to
work on a canvas. His efforts, of course, were futile; tears ran
down his cheeks. Lovingly the artist's wife laid her hand on the
boy's shoulder and spoke: "You will never be able to paint like
the great master unless you have his spirit."

Would you have the Master's touch as you handle the thorny
problems confronting your own life and the life of your generation? Having His words, gloriously true as they are and admiring
the Vision Splendid, are not enough. We must catch His Spirit.
Rather, His Spirit must catch us, capture and empower us.

PRAYER: *O Holy and Gracious Spirit, come Thou to us and fill
our whole being with Thy self. Give us quietness and courage,*

strength and kindliness, that we may grow into Thy likeness and go forward in Thy service.

Spirit of Light and Power, rekindle a heroic and mighty faith in the heart of Thy Church; let not the gates of Hell prevail against it. May it be baptized anew with the spirit of unity, the flame of vision, and the sacrificial passion of Christ. Amen.

17

Why the Church?

As His custom was, He went into the synagogue on the Sabbath day.
LUKE 4:16

WHEN Luke reports that Jesus announced His revolutionary program of the Kingdom in His home church at Nazareth, he adds a phrase which tells us much concerning the Master's own attitude toward the Church of His day. *"As His custom was, He went into the synagogue on the Sabbath day."* The synagogue was Judaism's equivalent of the Church. As such it was far from perfect. Jesus broke with many of its teachings, criticized its weaknesses and denounced the hollowness and harshness of some of its leaders. But He believed in it, made participation in its worship and teaching a habit of His life: He went to Church on the day dedicated to worship, "as He was accustomed to do." Subsequently the Gospels record His intention to build the Church with such spiritual strength that it would be impregnable to the assaults of life-destroying forces. His most famous follower was deeply moved by his Lord's love of the Church, so deep that He sacrificed Himself for her, gave Himself to make her in His eyes altogether glorious: "Christ loved the Church and gave Himself up for her."[1] "What did it cost," a friend asked Quinton Hogg, "to build the Polytechnic Institute of London?" "One man's life," was the answer. Building the Church was costly, too. One Man's life was given that its foundation might be laid secure. Many lives have been given to make the Church glorious in witness, service and holiness.

But of too few in every community can it be said that they go

140

to church as their custom is. Christlikeness is venerated; belief in God, we are assured by a recent survey, is fairly general. Christian ideals are acknowledged to be the noblest. But as for the Church —"Why the Church?" is a familiar response.

An excellent religious motion picture recently was shown, entitled *Reaching from Heaven*. Young people who take a low view of religious films that are ineptly done or overpious gave this particular film their approval. The situations and characters depicted were realistic. For example, one incident was woven around the efforts of two young workmen to make a date with an attractive young woman who worked in the office of their construction company. One, an avowed pagan, offered a day at the lake. He could hardly believe his ears when the other—a loyal churchman—gave his invitation: "How about a date to go to church with me next Sunday morning?" "Now I've heard everything," quipped the first young man. As for the young woman, brought up in a comfortable but secularized home, she laughed: "Why the Church?"

Why the Church? Significant groups in our society put the question contemptuously. There is no reason, they say—unless it is to keep up an old tradition, or on certain high festivals like Christmas and Easter, or at weddings and funerals, to observe social niceties. Marxists give their answer bluntly, savagely; repeating the old parrot phrases about religion being the opium of the masses, and worship a superstition and escape. The pagan capitalist gives much the same answer—without the same arguments!—by his indifference and absenteeism. So-called liberals in religion, the humanists, speak similarly; they talk condescendingly of church-ianity versus true Christianity, as if that were a true antithesis. As for many nominal church members, church attendance and support no longer represent a religious obligation. They believe in the Church, expect the Church to function, and to be there at the same old stand when a crisis occurs in family life. But to destroy any structure one does not need to use dynamite, or hammers and crowbars. Just quit living in it, working on it, maintaining it. The gnawing tooth of time, aided and abetted by termites and rot, will turn a thing of usefulness and beauty into a ruin.

You may be helped by considering the Christian answer to this question, Why the Church? An unpleasant experience in some church long ago may have soured you. You found a prominent church member, or even clergyman, to be a caricature of the creed he professed. You discovered that there were hypocrites in the same pew with you. Of course occasionally there might be one or two in the same row at the theater, but that is a different matter. Your criticism is a kind of compliment to the institution you have rejected; but you need to review your decision. You do not know what you are missing! And it will not do to say that active participation in a visible, local church does not matter so long as through your efforts to lead a good life outside you are a member of the Church Invisible. The Church Invisible is a reality, but it includes the Church visible, the Church militant and imperfect.

Why the Church?

Let me try to give you three reasons in the form of three questions: Why comradeship in the service of the best? Why faith? Why worship?

First, let us face the question, *Why comradeship in the service of the best?*

Is it not sufficient that an individual live his own life in such a manner that his own conscience will approve his choices, and his way of living? But choices and a way of living involve relationships with others. "Real life is meeting" others in various situations. Private integrity is admirable, but as long as we live in a world of persons we cannot live as isolated atoms. We need others. Only the stupid individualist deceives himself with the lie, "I can do without you." We were made for fellowship, and live stunted lives when we cut ourselves off from others. In the service we give to good causes, we are immensely helped as we join others of kindred mind and purpose. As for the highest concern of all, vital religious living, have we realized that there is no such thing as solitary religion in the New Testament? Of course personal commitment to God, personal spiritual disciplines such as prayer and the other practices by which our spirits are strengthened, are basic. Deep truth lies in the comment one thoughtful woman made to another: "Your religion's no good unless you can take it with two hands." The other agreed and recalled George Macdonald's saying: "Hold fast to God with one hand, and open wide the other to your neighbor. That is religion." Jesus vetoed the religion of the Priest and the Levite in His classic story of the good Samaritan. They were religious, but in the Master's eyes, their religion was a poor thing—it had only one hand. This is where the Church comes in. It provides fellowship in the highest aspirations and ministries. It is the School of Christ, and we have fellow students. It is the Army of the Lord, and we have the sustaining help of other soldiers. Strange, is it not, how we recognize this truth in other areas: we have found that in union there is strength in ranks of labor and management; in education, we prize the fellowship of learning—we have our schools and colleges; in science we have our research foundations and fellows. Yet so often in trying to live the good life, in matters of morality and spiritual experience and method, we try to go it alone. A Negro, asked what was wrong with his community, answered, "Well, the good ain't able, and the able ain't good." Through the Church the good become able, and together find resources to do what none can do adequately alone. Within the fellowship we find support for our noblest hopes. Jesus Himself acknowledged this need: To His comrades He said, "Ye are they which have continued with Me in My temptations." He gave us the secret of finding Him when He promised that "where two or three are gathered together" in His name—with His Spirit, true to His nature—there He will be in the midst.

The Church provides a fellowship above all others, transcending all differences of age, color, background—and Time itself. In reading his study of *God and Man*, I came across this startling declaration by Dr. Herbert Farmer of Cambridge: "The idea of the Church is part of the Christian doctrine of God." As God is love, and His purpose is to bring us back to life's true meaning, He calls into being, creates a new fellowship of men and women. This new community has for its distinctive mark all that we mean by Love—a love which makes no distinctions whatever, a love that goes out to men because they are there and because God loves them. Therefore the Church is not an optional addendum to the Christian way of life. It is not something which exists because of a social instinct; it is more than a club, even a very fine club. Thus runs the argument of this penetrating Christian thinker. Why the Church? Because the great God knows that only in the Body of Christ can we find our nourishment, our adventure, our healing, and dynamic to live according to His design.

Why the Church? Its necessity and significance shine with new clarity as we face our second question, *Why faith?*

Of course the Church has no monopoly in this matter of offering faith. On all sides there are rival institutions and movements —Marxian communism, secularism, materialism, this cult and that—dealing in the same commodity. Mr. T. S. Eliot in his famous poem, *The Rock*, describes the situation in these words:

> Men have left GOD not for other gods, they say, but for no
>   God; and this has never happened before
> That men both deny gods and worship gods, professing first
>   Reason,
> And then Money, and Power, and what they call Life, or Race,
>   or Dialectic.[2]

But the Church has no rival in the field of faith in the Christlike God, and in the supremacy of the Christlike life. Other religions express truth, Christianity *is* religion. That which was discovered partially by the noble founders of great religions has been revealed through Jesus Christ. Why the Church? A Scottish journalist made profession of his faith not long since, and was received as a communicant member. He was asked by his startled colleagues why he did so. His answer is worth pondering:

It is perhaps sufficient to say that I did not consider this to be a particularly appropriate time to stand on the touch-line and shout advice, far less a time to ignore the entire game. On the whole, I have never much admired people who could not apply headlines in their daily newspapers to their daily lives, and these appear to me to utter every morning a personal challenge to anyone who believes in what we are pleased to call our way of life.

Our way of life is a Faith, which issues in action. What is the Faith? That God not only lives, but that He has visited and redeemed His people in the historic person of Christ. That Jesus Christ is the cosmic message, the divine Word transmitted from the central broadcasting station of the Universe; that He is the Word made flesh. Man in his journeyings encounters the divine at many points—in nature, in history, in enlightened conscience, in creative genius, in good men and women. But these are imperfect, uneven "signals" so to speak. In Christ there is the authentic revelation. As we confront the total fact of Christ—His birth, His life, His teaching, His death, and His victory over death and abiding presence through the Spirit—we encounter the living God. We know that as Christ was so God is eternally. God takes the initiative, answering our need even before we call. He is our Creator, and our Redeemer. Do we need a redeemer? It is hard for us to admit it. Our pride balks at such an admission of our weakness and inadequacy. But soon or late life makes a breach in our defenses, and we know. Self-sufficiency comes a cropper, and our peace is shattered. We want to be forgiven, restored to the family, and know Peace. Then comes "the glorious news of our blessed God." There is forgiveness. There is reconciliation. God in Christ gave Himself on Calvary that we might know, that we might find in that divine sacrifice what we could find nowhere else: the action of God Himself to effect our release from the sense of unrelieved guilt, fear, despair. One tells of a man, a skeptic and anarchist who entered a church in Paris during the singing of Mass. The choir sang as ours does in the service of Holy Communion, "O Lamb of God, who takest away the sins of the world. . . !" Pierced by truth deeper than argument, the man went out into the street exclaiming, "O God! what a dream. If He only could!" But the Church declares that He does. The Church points to the Cross and declares that the Heart that forgives the brokenhearted must first be broken. Only out of that brokenness can wholeness come. All that is asked of us is to come, as penitent sinners, to trust that Love, accept Him, and obey. . . . *This Good News comes to you through the Church.* Remember that! Before the written Gospels, before the New Testament was written the Church existed, and the Church as custodian of the divine Facts provided the Gospels and Epistles under the inspiration of God's Spirit.

Why faith? Because "only the living flame of faith can scatter the night which has invaded the world without and the heart within." Because faith, the truest interpretation of reality which can be found, keeps life sane, holds it together, makes the week valiant, and maintains the moral health of the world. We were told that in Buchenwald concentration camp there was a poster prominently displayed which proclaimed: "HERE THERE IS NO GOD." They were wrong who said that, for God was there judging the beastly men and women who committed such unspeakable horrors on their fellows. Yet somehow, the person who put it up sensed that when men cease to believe in a God of holy and righteous love and no longer regard their lives as part of the divine drama, life itself degenerates into something foul and intolerable.

"Here there *is* God"—is the proclamation of the Church as it points to the world of persons. Here God discloses Himself in human terms, the Church affirms as it uplifts Christ.

Why the Church? Because within the Church lies the truth you and I need to discover, receive and apply. Because the Church is in actuality the Body of Christ, that through His grace we become incorporated into His mystical body—with the Spirit of Christ animating us, the Will of Christ operating through us, the Mind of Christ directing us, the Love of Christ sustaining us and encompassing us.

Why the Church? Here is the last question, the answer to which provides cogent reason for it and our part in it. *Why worship?* A short answer is this: we worship because we cannot help it. If a man will not worship God he will worship something, someone else. A human being must bow down to something. It may be the State, it may be Alcohol, Power, Collectivism . . . but a god he will have. Many still have the faith of secular humans of which Swinburne gave lyric expression: "Glory to man in the highest for man is the master of things!" Only such worshipers of *homo sapiens* are a little embarrassed when they consider how much man has failed to master—like war, famine, social relations and himself! Why worship? Because we need to get ourselves off our hands. Because we need to find a beam in the darkness; it is so easy to get lost in the world. Because we need constantly to renew our inner life at the Source of life; to confess our sorry misdoings and failure to do anything constructive; to be cleansed and renewed. Why worship? Because the end of a week finds us with power cut off, and we need to have the switches thrown in again, so that we can have light and power for the tasks which wait to be done. Through the Word and Sacraments comfort is found; we are made strong together with God and one another. Why worship? Because we need to be challenged by the call of our Lord "to fight the wrong that needs resistance, to help the cause that needs assistance, to serve the future in the distance."

> I do not ask for peace
> For life's eternal sorrow;
> But give me courage, Lord,
> To fight tomorrow![3]

Why the Church? Because to live life well, to have a life that is overflowing with meaning, quiet courage, deep joy, and unfailing usefulness—we need Comradeship in the experience and service of the best; we need a Faith to live by which furnishes both the reason and the dynamic for great living; we need Worship which will re-create us, cleanse and empower us.

Jesus "went into the synagogue on the Sabbath day, as His custom was." Christ loved the Church, and gave Himself for her in order to bring the Church to Himself in all her beauty, without a flaw or a wrinkle or anything of the kind, but to be consecrated and faultless.

PRAYER: *O Almighty God, who hast knit together Thine elect in one communion and fellowship in the mystical Body of Thy Son Christ our Lord: help us to make Thy Church the effective instrument of Thy purpose: that even as her Lord she may preach the Gospel to the poor, heal the broken-hearted, deliver the captive, recover sight to the blind, set at liberty them that are bruised, and preach the acceptable year of the Lord; through Jesus Christ, our Lord. Amen.*

18

Putting Things Right

> But he was angry, and would not go in: and his father came out, and entreated him. But he answered and said to his father, Lo, these many years do I serve thee, and I never transgressed a commandment of thine; and yet thou never gavest me a kid, that I might make merry with my friends: but when this thy son came, which hath devoured thy living with harlots, thou killest for him the fatted calf. And he said unto him, Son, thou art ever with me, and all that is mine is thine. But it was meet to make merry and be glad: for this thy brother was dead, and is alive again; and was lost, and is found.
>
> LUKE 15:28-32 (A.S.V.)

O NE of the major obstacles to putting things right in personal relationships with God and with others is the harsh and censorious attitude which good people take toward those who are not good. Jesus was sure of it. He Himself suffered more from the so-called righteous than from sinners. When the self-righteous, the proudly respectable, bristle with resentment toward those who have obviously strayed from "the straight and narrow," they, too, need to repent, and to be forgiven. For pride and an unforgiving spirit can work more havoc than riotous living.

This is why He told the story of the two brothers which we call the parable of the prodigal son. Certainly the younger son needed to put things right between himself and his father and the family. The main point of the story is the loving action of the heavenly Father to help him accomplish that. Jesus might have ended the story with the prodigal's penitent home-coming and the father's joyous welcome and pardon. Many wish He had ended the story there. But He went on and told about the elder brother who refused to surrender his resentment and rage against his wastrel brother, and his apparently lenient father. When this

149

elder son returned from work and learned why the party was being given, "he was angry and would not go in."

The simplest explanation of the story, of course, is that the father represents God, the younger brother the publican and sinners whom Jesus befriended, and the elder brother those scribes and Pharisees who criticized Jesus. What a mirror the last portrait presents to us!

The elder brother may wear our name. We, too, may keep the moral code, observe the proprieties, do our share of the work conscientiously. And yet we, too, may harbor resentments against others, whether younger or older, whom we feel have abused their position, squandered their substance, and in one way or another injured us. The elder brother's ideals were high. His sympathies were narrow. His resentment went deep. Therefore, said Jesus, he, too, needed to be set right.

"He was angry and would not go in." Wasn't it natural? Of course it was. One of the driving forces in every human being is this emotion of anger. Such a primitive force is easier to condemn than to eliminate. Asked to write an essay on Quakers, a boy wrote: "Quakers are very meek, quiet people who never fight or answer back. My father is a Quaker, but my mother is not." Few attain to the disciplined tempers of Quakers, but all of us can. Christ does not ask us to expel the powerful instincts and emotional drives which are part of our equipment. He does expect us to use them to serve the good purposes of God. He Himself was angry. Like Amos, the Old Testament prophet, He, too, urges us to "hate the evil, and love the good."[1] He whom we call the gentle Christ could flash out in indignation at impenitent wrong-doers. When He met the kind of person who was "hard as nails and cruel as hell" He said that it were better that a great mill-stone should be hanged about his neck and he be cast into the midst of the sea. "You are like whitewashed tombs," He said to some men He saw, "which outwardly appear beautiful, but within they are full of dead men's bones and all uncleanness."[2] Does this mean that He was angry against persons, that He retained His hatred of selfish and cruel men, that He was unforgiving? No. Always He hated the sin and loved the sinner. Always He went out in willingness to forgive.

A Christian is expected to be angry at whatever degrades human personality, and is expected to discipline that anger so that it can become an instrument to cure the evil condition. If we were never aroused we would be supine and spineless, we would be what a German thinker once described as "moral cows in our plump comfortableness."

Anger against an evil practice or condition can become righteous indignation. So as a young man Abraham Lincoln saw a human being auctioned off at a Southern slave market. It made him angry. He did not explode into a tantrum. It did not blind him to the complex character of the institution of slavery. Nor did it make him hate all Southerners. But he resolved that if ever the chance came he would hit the evil hard. The chance came. The result was the Emancipation Proclamation.

If only the prodigal-who-stayed-at-home had found a constructive outlet for his anger! He might have done something about those vicious temptations to which his brother succumbed. Best of all, he might have done something about himself, to make himself fit to live with; to keep the family spirit so alluring that whether his brother remained home or went away the beauty and strength of the family spirit would keep him from falling. For Rudyard Kipling was probably right in suggesting that the elder brother provided one reason why the younger left home. Jealousy, self-righteousness, harsh criticism speak in his complaint. Something like this might have been said by the younger fellow as he started out on his reckless and feckless career:

> I never was very refined, you see,
> (And it weighs on my brother's mind, you see)
> And there's no reproach among swine, d'you see,
> For being a bit of a swine.

So I'm off with wallet and staff to eat
The bread that is three parts chaff to wheat,
But glory be!—there's a laugh to it,
Which isn't the case when we dine.[3]

Many a person has been driven into a far country by the loveless-ness of an associate. Many a potentially useful citizen of the Kingdom of God has been "put off" taking his rightful place in the Church by the exclusiveness and pride he has found in church members.

How careful we must be to follow Jesus in this matter of our anger and indignation. If the elder brother had disciplined and directed his strong emotions into socially useful channels, he would have been healthier. For anger does things to us physically. It increases our strength. The old story has point. A wife asked her husband to go out and give their maid a good talking to; not because the domestic helper was unsatisfactory, but because Bridget always beat the carpets better when she was angry! But the energy released by such anger and resentment does not make us think more clearly. It actually distorts our vision. Dr. E. Stanley Jones tells of an optometrist who knew that anger disturbs vision. Being wise, this man applied his knowledge to himself. When-ever he became angry driving his car he drew to the side of the road until his anger cooled down. Who has not learned painfully that it is possible to become so "mad" that we cannot see straight? Today is Labor Day Sunday. We would not oversimplify the causes of labor-management disputes whereby both parties and the community as a whole suffer economic and social loss. Unjust practices ought to produce anger which expresses itself in re-sistance leading to reformation of unfair conditions. Evidence of the effectiveness of such a weapon is furnished in the history of the labor movement. Yet is it not true that such difficulties as exist today in industrial relations are frequently aggravated and prolonged by the unwillingness of one or both parties to sur-render their resentments and undertake negotiation from the high level of mutual understanding, respect and good will? Try to get even with an individual or a group, and you hurt yourself and your cause more than you do your opponent.

Legitimate anger can serve a high purpose. Jesus found Himself blocked by self-righteous Sabbatarians who objected to His healing sick persons on their holy day and he "looked around at them with anger, grieved at the hardness of their hearts."[4] His anger was grief; He was hurt that religious leaders could be so unjust and unmerciful. But Jesus taught the high cost of hating. He showed us what cherished resentments did to the elder brother. Life is made to work only on the basis of love which has a cross and a resurrection at the heart of it. Families divide, communities yield to racial and class prejudice, nations withdraw behind iron curtains and atomic bomb stock piles unconvinced that the loveless suspicious spirit of the elder brother cannot succeed in God's world.

How the character of a single person improves and his moral influence grows when he moves out of resentful into magnanimity! During World War II, Winston Churchill exhibited understandable anger at the Western nations' enemies and made it a powerful instrument for their defeat. His political adversaries in the House of Commons received from him measure for measure. One of his fellow members of Parliament, Mr. A. P. Herbert, tells how when hostilities had ended, and his leadership had been rejected by a majority of voters, many of his critics were won to admiration for him by the magnanimity he displayed toward them. Leaving the House of Commons one night in 1948, Mr. Churchill exchanged greetings with a small group gathered in the smoking room. His glance fell on Richard Stokes, Socialist member for Ipswich. Throughout the war Mr. Stokes had attacked Mr. Churchill fearlessly and continuously. He was a formidable enemy to Mr. Churchill and his ministers.

> Now Winston came back and put a hand on his shoulder and said, "Of course I've forgiven you. Indeed, I agree with very much that you are saying. . . . Very good." He moved a few paces and said, as if we might be surprised by what he had

said: "Such hatred as I have left in me—and it isn't much—I
would rather reserve for the future than the past." He beamed
again and moved off a pace or two, but stopped again; and
made that inimitable sound of his own, half grunt half chuckle,
and he said: "H'm. A thrifty and judicious disposal of bile."[5]

Let any man or group refuse to make such a "thrifty and judicious
disposal" of resentment and he pays for such refusal in many ways.
James Moffatt translated a verse from the Sermon on the Mount
in this startling way: "Whoever is angry with his brother without
cause will be sentenced by God."[6] In the silent processes of judgment, by inner frustration and conflict, we are sentenced. It is a
law of life: if we hate we become hateful; if we are resentful, we
become resented. Nursing our grievances, maintaining our proud
superiority and self-righteousness, we stumble in the dark. Dr.
E. Stanley Jones learned from a study of history that peace treaties
have lasted on an average only two and one-half years. His explanation is convincing: "They were founded on revenge. So the
universe upset them. They broke down fighting against reality.
You can have peace or revenge, but you cannot have both."[7]

Here then is the truth as it is in Jesus: *the only way we can
put things right is to take the way of the Cross.* What is this way?
It is the way of forgiveness. Jesus insisted on it in His teaching:
we are to forgive seventy times seven. We are to forgive as God
forgives us: "forgive us our trespasses, as we forgive them that
trespass against us." We are to copy God! Our Lord demonstrated
the power of it on Calvary. If we remain unforgiving we block
the channel down which the divine pardon seeks to come to us.
You say it is hard? It is sometimes as hard as the wood and nails
of the Cross. But it works. You say, "What if the person to be
forgiven is undeserving?" At the least, your offer of love will be
a bright spot on his way to hell! At the best, you never know how
God's Spirit will use your love to bring him to himself, home to
the Father, and to the family.

> I do not fear to walk the lonely road
> Which leads far out into the sullen night.

Nor do I fear the rebel, wind-tossed sea
  That stretches onward, far beyond the might
Of human hands or human loves. . . .
                                    It is
The hate-touched soul I dread, the joyless heart;
  The unhappy faces in the streets;
The smouldering fires of unforgiven slights.
  These do I fear.
Not Night, nor surging seas, nor rebel winds,
  But hearts unlovely, and unloved.[8]

My friends in an American city, a gifted Methodist minister
and his wife, had one son. He was a lad of great promise and
winsomeness. In World War II this boy served with the United
States Navy. During an engagement with the enemy he was killed
by a Japanese bullet. That Christian couple grieved as only loving parents can. If they experienced anger and resentment, swiftly
they surrendered their anger and resentment to Christ. They re-
dedicated their energies to the crusade for just and durable world
peace. They did more. To their own church, and to their own side,
they brought a Japanese minister and his family. When Brotherhood Week was observed in that community an editor paid tribute to them. Every week is brotherhood week in that church, he
said. Those disciples of the King of Love believe that a Christian
has no enemies. He may have critics, opponents, adversaries, but
no enemies. Why? Because a Christian has no enmity.

Listen: "The only possible way to get rid of an enemy is to turn
him into a friend, and the only possible way to turn him into
a friend is to forgive him."

Sometimes I imagine myself facing Christ. I acknowledge my
resentments, think I am doing quite well in getting rid of them.
"Lord," I say, "I will forgive but I won't forget." Christ's great
eyes search me. Then I know *that* is not enough. I try again:
"Lord, I will forgive, but I won't have anything to do with them."
Still those eyes, like X rays, penetrate my hardness. You hear Him
saying, from pain-drenched lips on Calvary, "Father, forgive
them. . . ." "Love one another, as I have loved you."

The good news for you and me who may be in the same class with that elder brother is this: the father came out to both. He ran out to the returning wanderer. "His father came out [to the angry elder brother] and entreated him . . . and he said unto him, 'Son [my dear boy], all that is mine is thine. Share in my joy. . . .' "

You and I want to help set things right in this topsy-turvy world, do we not? Let us begin where we are, as we are, even with those we are sure we never can like. We simply cannot help ourselves or anyone else if we shut ourselves out of heaven here or hereafter by our own lovelessness.

Since Jesus lived and since Jesus died on the Cross to make us sure of God's forgiving love, something new is operating in this world. It is "something transcending hatred, surpassing revenge or even just punishment"—it is the "miraculous extra" of love. Why not yield to it, to Him?

PRAYER: *Eternal Love, our Father, Thou hast forgiven us. Help us to forgive others, for Christ's sake and in His Spirit. Amen.*

19

Questions Before the House

Why do you call me Lord and not do what I tell you?   LUKE 6:46 (R.S.V.)

And He said to them, "Why are you troubled, and why do questionings rise in your hearts? See . . . It is I Myself. . . ."   LUKE 24:38 (R.S.V.)

AN INTERESTING discussion by diners in a Washington cafeteria was recently reported. The conversation theme was the decline of the old-fashioned Fourth-of-July celebrations, in which the day's fireworks ended with a bang and a whimper. A woman, described in official jargon as a "female research assistant in nuclear physics," revealed to her colleagues that she had once smoked a Roman candle. She was asked how she had gone about it, how the smoke tasted, how long she had been unconscious as the result of her experiment. "No one," commented Thomas Sugrue, who related the story, "asked her *why* she had done it."

When Mrs. John Q. Citizen reads in the newspaper or hears over the radio that the state or federal government, a church council, or an educational institution has decided to proceed with a certain policy, she is likely to ask her husband, "John, why are they going to do that?" Rising to the implied compliment to his superior knowledge but not to the question, John is likely to answer, "Oh, I suppose because they know how."

One of our forgotten words is the little three-letter "Why?" Despite its usefulness in preserving human rights and human lives, it is less and less used, even in democratic nations where no penalty is imposed upon the person who asks it. One exception must be noted. According to reliable reports from parents, children still use it with alarming frequency: "Why, Mom? Why?

Why?" But many a baffled and weary parent suspects it is often employed as a device to gain time and defer execution of an unwelcome order. Nevertheless, parental anxiety would be increased if children ceased asking questions beginning with "Why?" Failure to put such queries to their older companions and guides might indicate an unhealthy apathy, even arrested development.

When citizens and professing Christians refrain from putting and facing similar questions, the vitality of the body politic and the body spiritual may be perilously low. Of course there are other questions of importance than those seeking to know "For what?" Some years ago a beloved and gifted teacher of Protestant preachers told his colleagues that their forgotten word was "How?" The pulpit tends to be strong on exhortation and weak on instruction. We may be helpful in pointing out what to do and where to go and yet overlook the obvious question, "How to . . . ?" Today, however, "know how" is at the front of the procession. A veritable spate of "know how" books is available, many of them useful. Any person in quest of techniques whereby friends and customers may be won, peace of mind and soul gained, confidence and poise acquired, can pay his money and take his choice.

Let no one despise "know how." By our proficiency in this department ineptitudes and even insecurity may be conquered. No one who drinks her milk should take pot shots at a sacred cow, and all of us benefit from this particular one. Who would willingly return to the age of tallow candles, oxcart transportation, and the spinning wheel? Nevertheless, the time is here when we must give more serious attention to the issues wrapped up in "know why." Large exports of technological skills and the machinery produced by them will not convince victims of war and of totalitarian promises and threats that democracy is all that we know and claim for it, unless we know why, and tell them.

Did it ever occur to you that our Master used "Why?" repeatedly in His redemptive ministry to men? The first picture we have of Jesus in the Gospels, with the exception of the beautiful nativity scenes, is as an eager boy in the midst of the doctors of the law, both hearing and asking questions. You may be sure that some of His questions began with "Why?" Early He confronted men and women with disconcerting questions concerning accepted practices, hallowed customs and venerable institutions. "Why are you afraid?" "Why have you no faith?" "Why test me?" "Why callest thou Me good?" There are answers, and He wanted us to find them. The Supreme Teacher believed that nothing in the true education matters so much as asking the right questions of the right persons.

Authentic Christianity encourages questions, and provides the most adequate answers to the questions most worth asking. Does this mean that a Christian has "all the answers"? Far from it; but it does mean that the Christian receives light in the dark of life's mystery sufficient to rise out of confusion and doubt. For in seeking, in asking, the Christian receives Him who is both Truth and Life.

There are questions before the house—your house and mine, the house of man's soul. Think of two which Christ asked, and which He still asks of His followers. The first is this:

"Why do you call Me Lord and not do what I tell you?" Does this mean that we are not to acknowledge His lordship? Who that knows anything of His character and transforming power can do otherwise than accord Him the supreme place? For myself I find no category adequate to contain Him. In His presence I am moved to adoration. Like another who must have known many intellectual doubts, I can do no other than to call Him "my Lord and my God" incarnate in human personality. Jesus our Lord knew too much about human nature to imagine that confronted by Him we would not call Him by the highest name. Yet as another has said, He knew the peril of worshiping Him divorced from obedience to Him. Adulation without emulation is not enough; it may insulate the personality against the full impact of His Spirit. No true leader seeks personal admiration but rather implementation of his principles and ideals. Following Abraham Lincoln's tragic death a wave of veneration for him swept across our country. Such hero worship was inevitable. Almost simultaneously some of the men who vied with one another in paying tributes to the martyred President advocated a policy toward the South diametrically opposed to that for which Lincoln stood and for which he pleaded. In sorrow and indignation the spirit of the magnanimous statesman might have asked, "Why call me great, why hail me as the Great Emancipator if you do not do the things I wanted done?"

Christ, our divine Leader and Redeemer, is to be reverenced and adored. He is also to be obeyed by those who acknowledge Him "the mightiest among the holy and the holiest among the mighty." We are to "try His works to do," the things which He commanded. By such obedience others shall know that we are indeed His disciples. What things? The main outline of His program has been clearly set forth. His way for us and for our time can be discerned. By intelligent study of His teachings in the New Testament, by learning how His ethic and His dynamic must operate in the human situation we confront and in which we participate, by inward reliance upon His Spirit through prayer, we can know.

"What things, Lord?" I ask Him.

"Seek ye first the Kingdom of God"—the community of right relationships with the Father and with all members of His human family—"and all these things"—security, peace, inner satisfaction—"will be added unto you."

"What things, Lord?"

"Love one another." How much? "As I have loved you."

"What things, Lord?"

"Forgive one another, seventy times seven." In His arithmetic that means, not four hundred and ninety times, but world without end!

"Take up your cross daily, deny yourself, and follow Me." A cross is something more than stoical endurance of a toothache, or even the gallant acceptance of an inescapable disability. A cross means the voluntary shouldering of a burden you can avoid, but which you get under and carry for Christ's sake and for the sake of others.

"What things, Lord?"

"Feed my sheep. Feed my lambs." But if this means actual food, continued economic assistance to entire nations, have we not done more than our share? Will it not jeopardize our own standard of living, and add to already painfully high taxes? He who looked with compassion on the needy multitude looks deep into our souls and through our specious reasons: "Ye call me Lord, and ye do well, but why . . . ?"

The second question before our house leads us, as Scottish folk say, "far ben," deeply into, the truth of the Gospel. On the first Easter evening this question was asked by the Risen Christ of His intimate followers. The inner circle had gathered at the old rendezvous. Incredible reports had reached them that the slain Leader had triumphed over death. Perhaps it was a kind of hallucination. Even while they mulled over the testimony, Jesus Himself stood among them. St. Luke reports Christ's first words to the astonished men: "Why are you troubled and why do questionings rise in your hearts? See . . . it is I Myself. . . ."

"Why do questionings rise in your hearts?" Why not? Who would remain untroubled by racking doubts that had seen the divinest hopes come crashing down around a gaunt bloodstained cross? Had I been there I would have had depressing questions, and so would you. Is this the kind of world in which the best is always at the mercy of the worst? What shall it profit to vote and toil and sacrifice for a more excellent way of living if the unregenerate possessors of power have the last word? But the fact of Christ's resurrection discloses the true nature of reality. At the heart of this mysterious universe the Christlike lives. The God of holy, righteous love who has declared His invincible purpose in Jesus Christ has the last word, and that word is victory. Since God is for us when we are for the best we know, who can be against us?

We are troubled; who could be otherwise that knows the state of the world and the condition of our own souls? Yet He points forward, even while He directs our attention to Himself. "See, within the community of believers, the Body of Christ, it is I Myself."

In *Crusade in Europe* General Eisenhower relates a moving incident connected with the crossing of the Rhine River on March 23 and 24 of the last year of World War II. The assault on enemy positions was preceded by a violent bombardment in which two thousand guns of all types participated.

> Meanwhile infantry assault troops were marching up to the water's edge to get into the boats. We joined some of them and found the troops remarkably eager to finish the job. . . . Nevertheless, as we walked along I fell in with one young soldier who seemed silent and depressed.
>
> "How are you feeling, son?" I asked.
>
> "General," he said, "I'm awful nervous. I was wounded two months ago and just got back from the hospital yesterday. I don't feel so good!"
>
> "Well," I said to him, "you and I are a good pair then, because I'm nervous too. But we've planned this attack for a long time and we've got all the planes, the guns, and airborne troops we can use to smash the Germans. Maybe if we just walk along together to the river we'll be good for each other."
>
> "Oh," he said, "I meant I was nervous; I'm not any more. I guess it's not so bad around here." And I knew what he meant.[1]

"Why are you troubled? Why do these questionings arise in your heart?" Could it be that you have forgotten that He has planned the attack on the enemy for a long time, that His resources are sufficient to achieve complete victory? Our Divine Commander speaks this inspiriting word: "I am with you alway. . . . Let us walk along together."

PRAYER: *Keep us ever on the line of discovery, O Lord, that the truth we most need to know may be revealed to us. Let Thy Spirit disturb our consciences by uncovering the needs of our fellow*

*men and by calling us to help Thee meet them with intelligence,
courage and devotion. So may we love Thee with all our minds,
hearts, souls and strength, and our neighbors as ourselves, in the
faith and friendship of our invincible Lord, even Thy Son Jesus
Christ. Amen.*

20

The Necessity of Comradeship

If thou wilt go with me, then I will go: but if thou wilt not go with me, then I will not go. And she said, I will surely go with thee. . . .   JUDGES 4:8, 9

ONE of the famous patriots of ancient Hebrew history was a woman, Deborah. Her exploits are lyrically set forth in the Book of Judges. This Old Testament Book of Judges preserves the kind of tribal narratives of heroes which would run from mouth to mouth within a particular tribe. The "Judges" were not in the least like our modern magistrates and administrators. They were "tribal leaders, called upon to solve the many and varied problems of social life that were bound to arise and, in addition, to maintain where they could the religion of Jehovah." Outstanding men, imposing in stature, successful in military campaigns, would naturally be chosen. It was a time of "blood and iron," of violence and cruelty. We are surprised to discover among these leaders a woman. Even in that far-off era it is evident there was no such person as a "mere" woman. Deborah must have been a commanding personality, vigorous of mind, resourceful, brave. Her country's Canaanitish enemies had harassed the settlers for twenty years. Under the able leadership of the commander Sisera, the foe had rumbled their devastating way into the little groups of Israelites in the north. What could they do? Meager equipment, pitifully inadequate arms, heavy losses among their "effectives," destroyed harvests, all combined to destroy hope. In that crisis Deborah supplied the impulse that saved the nation. Her daring plan involved massing the clansmen on Mount Tabor, and from that summit hurling an attack on Sisera. She called Barak to rally the troops. But Barak was unwilling to proceed on this enterprise without the companionship of Deborah. His words come across the centuries a memorable expression of the truth that comradeship in high endeavor is a necessity: "If thou wilt go with me, then I will go: but if thou wilt not go with me, then I will not go. And she said, I will surely go with thee." The massed attack of Barak's men was successful. The forces of nature seemed to take sides with Barak and Deborah in his bold onslaught. Sisera had to contend not only with an army trained in secret, but with the river Kishon overflowing its banks. Never again did the Canaanites trouble the Israelites. Comradeship in the service of the nation, undergirded by simple, powerful religious faith brought off the victory.

Comradeship is a necessity for success on any field of battle. Two opposing armies may have almost equal amounts of equipment, training, experience. Commanders of both forces may be equally skillful. Allowing for unpredictable factors of weather and terrain, it is reasonable to assume that the army to emerge victorious will be that which has the greater unity of purpose, the most real sense of comradeship among officers and men. Comradeship based on shared experience and shared faith is essential in any significant task. "If thou wilt go with me, then I will go: but if thou wilt not go with me, then I will not go."

If you turn to the Bible you find that this truth lights its pages from end to end, leading from a Garden to the City of God. Certainly the New Testament knows little of private, solitary religion. Think of only two expressions of this conviction. In the words of Jesus: "Where two or three are gathered together in My name, there am I in the midst." From the First Epistle of John: "If we walk in the light as He is in the light, we have fellowship—comradeship—one with another." What the Bible underlines and celebrates, our human experience attests as true:

> Fellowship is heaven,
> Lack of fellowship is hell.

For one thing, *comradeship is a necessity in order to become a real person.* "To be is to be in relations." How commonly we recognize this fact when we speak of its opposite. We do not approve of a child retreating from people, or of an acquaintance shrinking into his shell. We know that there is something that does not like a wall—a wall which isolates a person in lonely individualism. "The something" is the spirit of life itself. Loneliness everyone knows at one time or another, but by a sound instinct we diagnose chronic loneliness as a symptom of a spiritual ailment which ought to be cured, and which can be cured by Adventures in Friendship. Thackeray once said, "How lonely we are in the world! how selfish and secret, everybody! . . . Ah, sir, a distinct universe walks about under your hat and under mine— all things in nature are different to each . . . you and I are a pair of infinite isolations, with some fellow-islands a little more or less near us." But if we are thus isolated we are not likely to grow into mature persons. "Full-grown personality involves the blending of lives." Does this mean that I am pleading that we love one another? Yes, but not sentimentally, and not because as a minister I am expected to say it. I ask that we regard comradeship no longer as an option which we may take up or lay down as we please; but as a requirement of real living. "For my part," said Rowland Hill out of his isolation, "I long to fall in with somebody. This picket duty is monotonous. I hanker after a shoulder on this side and on the other." Of course! We work better, we play better, we pray better in fellowship. Look at the growth of clubs, cults, guilds, crafts, fraternities! They reveal how insistent, deep and passionate is the hunger for comradeship. The arts require it, from the Group of Seven artists to an academy. Universities are fellowships of learning. Because of this, the Church is indispensable. On the human side it is founded on one of human nature's basic urges. Self, sex, the herd are described as the three fundamental drives within us. The herd or social drive is frustrated unless the individual works out his spiritual life in a corporate fellowship. How impoverished we remain if we meet as neighbors or associates or friends in business, in community projects, in recreation, but never or rarely ever as children of the Highest, comrades in the spiritual life. This comradeship within the Kingdom of God the Church must foster and develop. Never must barriers of narrow creed or rite debar men from "the fellowship of the mystery." Paul longed to "be comforted together with you by the mutual faith of you and me." So men and women immersed in the tasks and trials of life in a world like this long to be comforted, to be completed, to be healed of every type of hurt, within the community of Christ, within the comradeship of Christ's Good Companions. Today, thanks be to God who is the author of fellowship, around the world the great Church prays as never before:

> Gather us in, Thou Love that Fillest all!
> Gather our rival faiths within Thy fold
> Rend each man's temple veil and bid it fall,
> That we may know that Thou has been of old;
> Gather us in![1]

Good neighbor, "if thou wilt go with me, then I will go" into satisfying experience; "but if thou wilt not go with me"—or if I will not go with thee—then neither of us shall become the real persons the Divine Friend intends us to become.

Consider, too, that *comradeship is a necessity if we are to outwit evil*. Global war has proved that, written it in letters of fire and blood. Divide and conquer has ever been the strategy of evil forces. To us in Church as in the United Nations the Spirit of God calls. Unite to overthrow tyrants and save the dear values of common life. Genuine response to such a challenge has been the open secret of freedom. "Marching along together" with a friend whose confidence in us never wavers, evokes the best in us, makes us "more than conquerors" over once frightening foes. That is why it is a devil's stratagem to sow distrust of allies in our minds.

World Communion Sunday celebrates the fact that every Christian and every Christian congregation has innumerable allies in the Church of Christ on earth and in heaven. World Communion Sunday also stabs our consciences broad awake to the sin of our divisions within the Body of Christ. Can a divided Church speak authoritatively the word God gives it to speak? Is a divided Church likely to convince a divided world that unity of the Spirit in Christ is not only desirable but attainable in our time? Has it occurred to us that one of the reasons the churches of a community exert relatively little influence on social and political groups who need to be influenced for some civic good is that the separate churches proceed separately? Dr. Edwin T. Dahlberg of St. Louis once told of a coach of a Midwestern university football team who underscored the necessity of team play for more than his players. His team had lost seven games in succession. After the last defeat he spoke with disarming restraint to the disappointed players: "Boys, you have had a remarkably successful season. You all played magnificently—every man in his position. *The trouble was in the spaces between your positions. That's where our opponents came through.*" On the whole we who comprise the members of this city's churches also have had a fairly successful season. We have engaged in some study of the complex society in which we function; have passed a few relevant resolutions, and forwarded them to our representatives in local and federal government. New recruits for Christ and the Church have been won. As Baptists, Congregationalists, Episcopalians, Methodists, Presbyterians, we have each played at times magnificently, every church in its own position. "The trouble was in the spaces between our positions. That's where our opponents came through."

When it comes to outwitting the evil temptations and habits which reduce our effectiveness, the same truth applies. Sin may well be "the voluntary choosing of the worse instead of the better." Down in the depths where we make our choices an evil thought takes possession of our imaginations, and before we know it our will is overpowered. What then? Are we to try alone to overcome this tendency to choose the "easy low" instead of "the hard high"? How hopeless becomes solitary attack on some fear, some habitual weakness. We try to deal with our moral enemy alone. It is an unequal struggle. How does a person achieve deliverance and mastery? It is through comradeship with a good person. Such comradeship grows as we trust him to reinforce our desire. We go forward together not simply to direct attack on the thing we fear, the thing which has overcome us; we go forward together into new attitudes and activities. In place of an actual head-on engagement with evil you and he put a positive program of goodness. Dr. Fosdick wrote in his helpful book, *On Being a Real Person,* "This world has some great people in it to believe in." Indeed it has, and towering above all others is the Supreme Person, Christ. You were meant for friendship with Him! He is called "the friend of publicans and sinners." "You are My friends," He says, "if you do whatsoever I command you." "I have called you friends, for all things that I have heard from My Father, I have made known to you." Religion, according to our Lord, is friendship with God and with one another in Him. We never outwit "the evil we do by being us" until we realize this divine Friend's forgiveness. Forgiveness is real, and available, in this Friend. By experiment, we know that God receives sinners. He draws us back to His heart. He says to the man who kneels at the Cross, "My Son, let us share the sorrow of it all and live down the shame together." He is willing to suffer in order to bring about forgiveness. The inevitable suffering for forgiveness' sake was laid on God also, on Him most of all, and His response to the tragic need is Calvary. In Jesus' passion we see the pardoning agony of the Father. "Have you seen," once asked the great Scottish scholar Hugh R. Macintosh, "that the Cross was your Unseen Friend making overtures to you—opening the door, that you might come in and ask to be forgiven?" Sober, verifiable truth is the old hymn:

> I've found a Friend; O such a friend!
> He bled, He died to save me;
> And not alone the gift of life,
> But his own self He gave me.

The Saviour of men speaks today as in all the days gone by, pointing to the eternal Calvary where God's pardoning friendship outwits and forgives every moral failure: "If thou wilt go with me, then I will go: ... I will surely go with thee."

Comradeship is necessary to become a real person, to complete our selves; friendship with the best is essential to the mastery of evil. If these propositions are true—and from our own experience we know them to be gloriously true—then it follows that *comradeship is necessary if we are to make the future good and great.* What can heal the old wounds of racial and religious differences but a new comradeship, based on a just recognition of each group's diverse traditions and beliefs? No sensible citizen seeks a mere "mush of concessions," but a new league of friendly minds within the nation. No realistic churchman advocates reunion of the churches for the sake of creating a huge, efficient, economically sound enterprise. But every perceptive churchman knows that God's will is for a United Church of Christ.

For what does a democratic nation such as ours exist? To become one of the chief economic powers of the world? To be a pioneer in achieving maximum social security for all who live within its borders? Is that all? Or does it exist primarily to fulfill God's holy purpose to build within the new world a Beloved Community united, just and free, where men of every race and creed may live and live well? Are we not sent to the Kingdom for such a time as this, that we may demonstrate that Christ's prayer is the only practical statesmanship for all peoples: "that they all may be one"; one in spirit and in purpose: the spirit that of God's family, "the whole family in heaven and earth." Friends, we were made for comradeship! We resist the undefeatable purpose of God when we strive against such friendship. Only in comradeship with the Christ of all souls shall we learn the wisdom, acquire the power, practice the way by which today and tomorrow shall be good and great. Dr. T. R. Glover in a study of the Roman emperor, Marcus Aurelius, uncovered the source of his fundamental failure when he said, "He does not believe enough to be great." Do you believe enough? Will you trust this Friend to enlarge your belief in the attainable greatness of His design for the Church and for the world? Will you strike out, brave the hazards and give yourself to the Christian crusade? This does not mean that we shall merely sweeten stubborn and complex situations with friendliness. Nor does it mean that we shall go about our world-rebuilding "blind." Jesus said that kindness can be wasted on brutal men as pearls before swine. But comradeship on the Christian level is the key to any hopeful future for humanity. All people are intermeshed, crowded together, so that if mankind is to exist at all it must exist in terms of creative positive friendship. You can begin where you are, pushing out your friendship across embittered barriers of creed and class, nation and race.

Face the urgent problems of becoming a satisfying kind of person, of outwitting the evil around us and within us, of becoming active soldiers of Christ for the sake of our world's future and you will feel how little you can do without the enabling, liberating and gladdening power of God our Friend. It is told of Robert Bruce, the great preacher of the days of James VI, that no man spoke with such evidence and power of the Spirit. Dr. Adam Burnet has retold the story. "No man," the record runs, "had so many seals of conversion; yea, many of his hearers thought that no man, since the apostles, spake with such power." The secret of that unique inspiration is unveiled by what happened at Larbert in Scotland when he was in the vestry before service. Someone was sent to call him, but returned saying he did not know when he would be free to come, that "there was Somebody with him, for he heard him many times say with the greatest seriousness, 'that he would not, he could not go, unless He came with him, and that he would not go alone,' but the Other did not seem to answer," at least audibly. They said of him when he came out at last to preach, that "he was singularly assisted." "If thou wilt go with me, then I will go: but if thou wilt not go with me, then I will not go. And He said, I will surely go with thee. . . ."

PRAYER: *O Thou Great Friend of all the sons of men, the comrade of the beaten and broken, of the young and old, the valiant and the timid, bring us within the circle of Thy love and power and wisdom, that we may be to others what Thou art to us, the Unfailing Companion, the cup of strength to souls in need, the reconciling Friend.*

As we sit at Thy table and meditate upon Thy love for all the world, let our holy communion be in truth within the worldwide community of Thy holy Church. Draw us closer to Thyself and so closer to one another in Jesus Christ Thy Son our Saviour. Amen.

21

The "Thin Thread of Thanks"

Always give thanks for everything to God our Father, as followers of our Lord Jesus Christ.   EPHESIANS 5:20 (Goodspeed)

GILBERT KEITH CHESTERTON told us his life story a few years ago. In it he revealed the secret by which he recovered the reality and radiance of vital religion. Like many young people he had become muddled and confused, "not knowing what to do with life or what to make of it." It was a time when the sea of faith swirled in ebb tide and many a soul's ship lay high and dry on shoals of doubt and unbelief. Here is the clue which made a profound difference in the young Chesterton: "I hung on to the remains of religion by one thin thread of thanks. I thanked whatever god might be because any life lived at all." He "took life for gratitude, not for granted." He did not expect of life more than life had to give. He refused to whine or repine because there was so little good; he relished the good which existed. The tenuous "thin thread of thanks" led him into ampler, more zestful living.

If only you and I could find that "thin thread of thanks," cling to it, and follow it! We would find ourselves moving into newness of life, exchanging our feeble limping walk for a confident march to triumphant music and proud banners. We might even experience a blaze of wonder which would transfigure the common days.

Therefore on this Thanksgiving Sunday, to use William Blake's lines,

> I give you the end of [this] golden string,
>   Only wind it into a ball,

It will lead you in at Heaven's gate,
Built in Jerusalem's wall.

"The Lord knows we need something!" is a common lament. The world looks grim, the future at times appalling. Reporting the wedding of the present Queen Elizabeth and the Duke of Edinburgh a few years ago, the English novelist Rebecca West justified its pageantry by saying: "It was wise enough. People are tired of sadness, they need a party; they are tired of hate, they need to think of love; they are tired of evil, they need to think of goodness." People are indeed tired and a change of mental gears is demanded. For this is an age of anxiety, and our emotional uneasiness hangs itself on many hooks: the Bomb, the power of labor, the reaction of management, the ineptitudes of government, the ambiguous fact of Russia, the next depression. It may be that our fearfulness and depression are in direct proportion to our privilege and comfortableness. If your literary diet includes *The New Yorker,* you will recall a summer issue's cartoon showing a well-dressed woman sitting in an easy chair in a sumptuous resort hotel, exclaiming, "Wouldn't this be perfect—if it wasn't for Russia!" Vague fears gnaw at our peace, and often lead to foolish action or more foolish inaction. One proved antidote for pessimism and despair is the attitude of gratitude. "Always give thanks for everything to God our Father," urges St. Paul. Life for him was grim. For every one of his comrades in the little army of Christ the tomorrows looked rugged and ragged. They followed One whose life had ended on two wooden slabs uplifted on an ancient hill. Christ had promised no perfect existence for men and women who trudged along with Him; He did promise and give something infinitely better: abiding and unquenchable joy. And His ablest interpreter was sure that they would never find it by concentrating on the liabilities and losses, the deprivations and defeats. "Always give thanks for everything to God our Father, as followers of our Lord Jesus Christ."[1]

I

Grasp the "thin thread of thanks" and follow it into personal happiness. How much easier it is to live with individuals who cultivate the grace of appreciation than with those who act as though every day ends with a "bang and a whimper." To discuss the origin of Thanksgiving Day with Americans may seem as unprofitable as carrying coals to Newcastle or livestock to Chicago. But most North Americans tend to regard the "saints and strangers" who founded New England as for the most part difficult and dour. In any group that takes life's issues seriously there are bound to be those who become excessively solemn and severe. Among such pilgrim fathers and mothers the institution of Thanksgiving Day must have come as a sweetening and liberating influence. You recall from schooldays how the festival of remembrance of all God's mercies originated. When the colonies were first planted, settlers endured many privations. Being devoutly religious they laid their distresses before God on days of fasting and prayer. Continual meditation on such topics tended to make them gloomy and discontented, even disposed some to return to England. At last, when it was proposed to appoint still another day of penitence and humiliation, a sensible old colonist said that he thought that they had brooded over their misfortunes long enough; that it seemed high time they should remember all God's mercies to them. After all, in spite of adversity, they enjoyed happy homes, growing strength, civil and religious liberty, and above all the great salvation Christ had won for them. He proposed, therefore, that instead of a fast they should keep a feast. His advice was taken, and from that time Thanksgiving Day has been an annual observance in America.

Certainly, the person who "gives thanks for everything" is a more amiable companion in any colony than his opposite number. When unspoiled by overindulgence and luxury, children are spontaneously and genuinely grateful. A little girl of eight sum-

mers whom I know was asked by her teacher to compose a little
prayer of thanksgiving. This was the result, which is typical of
childhood's response:

> Thank You for our mothers, and for our fathers and sisters
> and brothers, and thank You for our homes and food and our
> clothes and thank You for the trees and flowers and animals
> and birds, and the winter time and the summer time. And O
> God bless all the little children and make them better when
> they are sick, and thank You for the sunshine and for the rain
> and the snow and the lovly [sic] skies, and thank You for the
> fields and mountins [sic], and make me a good little girl for
> Jesus sake. Amen.

"Natural Christians" of even a few years need no apostolic exhortation "always to give thanks for everything to God." "Except
ye turn, and become as little children" in gratitude as in trust,
you cannot enter into the kingdom of happiness. Learning and
other acquisitions of mature living need not destroy childlike-
ness in such matters. Harvey Cushing's biography contains that
noble surgeon's transcript of a prayer offered by President
Wheelock of Dartmouth College in 1798:

> O Lord, we thank Thee for the Oxygen Gas; we thank Thee
> for the Hydrogen gas; and for all the gasses. We thank Thee
> for the Cerebrum; we thank Thee for the Cerebellum; and for
> the Medulla Oblongata. Amen!

II

As we follow the "thin thread of thanks" we are led deeper
into durable joy because our kindled gratitude stimulates us to
share "all the blessings of this life" with others. So many are
hard bestead by misfortune and driven to practical atheism by
brutal circumstance.

Lacking appreciation of the sheer miracle of life, of its essential
and potential greatness, we are apt to miss a fundamental truth:
that life is a field of honor on which it is intended by the Lord
of all that we should be expendable for the sake of others. On a
recent Sunday an elderly servant of the servants of God came to

my vestry and shyly informed me that he had to tell someone of
the thrill which had come to him through giving what he called
a little time and money for sending food to Britain and Europe.
"You'll never believe how light my heart feels now!" he said. "You
know, the Master had something when He said, 'It is more blessed
to give than to receive'! I'm so thankful to have a share in it."
A Christian is one who cares, a Christian is one who shares, because he is unspeakably thankful for all he has received, and of
which he is trustee and transmitter. May I tell you what has
thrilled your Canadian neighbors "no end" as our English cousins
say, among recent events in the Republic? It has been the story
of a train, not the Train of Tomorrow (though that must be a
commuter's dream of celestial transportation) nor even the Freedom Train, inspiring as that eloquent reminder of our dearly
bought and dearly maintained liberties is to us all. It has been
the Friendship Train, in which Americans from coast and prairies
gave practical expression to their humanity and fraternity. As
those freight cars of food rolled across the land, they led a great
number of God's needy children to give praise for great and generous American hearts. Reverently, and without any desire to
pun, I say, "O God, may grace be given to us to follow in that
Train!" Gratitude can lead individuals and entire communities
to join the human race.

One of our noble American rabbis is my source for the story
of Sadie Virginia Smithson. Sadie lived in Johnson Falls, Virginia,
just prior to World War I. She was then an unknown, drab seam-
stress. She grew up there, and her major disappointment was her
discovery in young womanhood that she was unacceptable to the
local social circles. Her absorbing ambition was to become a member of the Laurel Literary Society. But her father kept a livery
stable, and she made clothes for a living. Frustrated in her desire,
she saved and scraped sufficient money to take a trip to Europe.
She felt sure that since no other Virginia Falls' resident had made
a grand tour she would be asked to lecture on her trip and even
to join the ranks of the elite, when she returned. Her visit coin-

cided with the outbreak of war. She was caught in Belgium. An Army officer offered to drive her to Paris so that she might board the boat train and return home. On the way, the driver became lost and they found themselves presently crossing a battlefield. As the car came to a stop, Sadie heard a young soldier in the shadows, crying, "Water, for God's sake, water!" Before she knew what she was doing, Sadie was out helping. She found a nearby spring, used her drinking cup to assuage the thirst of the man and of other wounded soldiers. Throughout the night she went around alone, binding up wounds with bandages made from her skirt, scribbling last messages for men who would be among the un-returning. With the first glimmer of dawn, an ambulance drew near. A young medical officer saw her and shouted, "Who are you, and what in thunder are you doing here?" "I am Sadie Virginia Smithson, and I have been holding hell back all night." Later on shipboard, Sadie recounted her incredible story to a friend. Her friend remarked, "Well, the Laurel Society will surely be glad enough now to have you belong." Sadie looked puzzled for a moment, then said: "But you don't understand. I've been face to face with war and death and hell and God. I've been born again. Do you reckon any of these little things matter now?" "What does matter?" "Nothing," she answered, "nothing but God and love and doing things for folks."

Take the "thin thread of thanks" for life, for being here in such a crucial age, for having the opportunity to help, to hold back hell and uphold the rule of heaven on earth!

III

The "thin thread of thanks" leads us into more satisfying personal living; it stimulates us to enter into mutually enriching relationships with others. It leads us, as Chesterton discovered, into the assurance that "the heart of the Eternal is most wonderfully kind." Immense and immeasurable benefits are given us which we did not create, could not earn nor deserve. The gifts of life and love and their rich revealings argue the existence of a supreme

Giver. Katherine Mansfield, brilliant literary artist, compelled for health's sake to seek a home in Switzerland, found herself rejoicing in the tonic mountain air and the loveliness of forest in summer. She wrote to a friend: "If only one could make some small grasshoppery sound of praise to *someone*—thanks to *someone*. But who?" Sixty years earlier, Leslie Stephen, who had parted with Christianity, lost his wife. He began a sentence to Lowell, "I thank"—then, recollecting that he had none to whom he could think himself indebted, he wrote: "I thank—something—that I loved her as heartily as I know how to love." Here are persons who makes a religious response to life, even though they think they have abandoned religious faith. Thankfulness assisted such souls to retain sanity and to discharge their duties. Is such a response of gratitude without foundation? We cannot think so; rather we believe, with Henry Sloane Coffin, that such persons, gracious in humility and thankfulness, are "the products of a gracious Being, with whom, whether they can name Him or not, their sensitive souls are in correspondence." Such thankfulness is an adjustment which man at his sanest makes to Reality.

How dreadful it would be (wrote Rossetti, the poet) if we had no one to thank for all the glorious things of life, as if they just happened. But we have Someone, of whose mercy we have had large experience: the God and Father of our Lord Jesus Christ. His huge bountifulness planned and secured "all this goodly crowded heritage." Arthur John Gossip has written a trenchant study of prayer.[2] In one of the chapters he asks, "What ought to be the main mood, dominating Christian worship, giving it tone and atmosphere?" He answers: "The prevailing note of Christian worship ought to be that joyous and exultant thanksgiving to God. That first; that most; that all in all. Are we not children gathering about our Father? And ought we not to come to One of whose love we are sure, with sunny faces, and with spirits that keep breaking into singing?" Are we not here as men and women on the road to Christlikeness, "to celebrate our deliverance by Christ, for the first time, or for the thousandth time"? Would anyone be drawn to our glorious Lord, as Augustine was drawn, by a certain seemly hilarity in our faith? Those much maligned Puritans whose sour-faced austerity is constantly lampooned—those were the men who insisted that the prayer of thanksgiving be brought back to the liturgy. "In everything give thanks," they said with Paul; "for this is the will of God for you," this is the mind and attitude He desires in us.

Is it not like our wonderful God that He regards it as signal service when we turn to Him with grateful spirits to give thanks for all He is, for all that He has done, is doing, and is forever giving that we might live more abundantly? "Whoso offereth praise, glorifieth Me."

> I give you the end of a golden string,
>   Only wind it into a ball,
> It will lead you in at Heaven's gate,
>   Built in Jerusalem's wall.

PRAYER: *O Most Loving Father, who willest us to give thanks for all things, let the grace of appreciation of all that Thou art and hast done and art doing for us and for all men stir us to praise Thee. With hearts unfeignedly thankful for our creation, preservation, and redemption in Jesus Christ, grant us such cheerful and complete commitment to Thy service, that we shall show forth Thy praise, not only with our lips, but in our lives; through Jesus Christ, Thine unsurpassed gift and our only Saviour. Amen.*

22

How to Be Popular with
the Best People

*They that fear Thee will be glad when they see me; because I have hoped in
Thy word.*   PSALM 119:74

LET me put a personal question to you. It may sound better
suited to a course on how to make friends and influence
customers. Are you popular with the best people? It is a good
question to ask ourselves. You have a right to say, it depends on
what you mean by the best people. From a Christian perspective
the best people are not necessarily those once quaintly designated
as "the four hundred," the socially prominent members of a
metropolitan or national community. By the best people we do
not mean those who give the best parties, nor those whose
appearance in a local banking institution evokes warm approval
in the minds of the directors. Are not the best people those with
whom we are at our best?

It is a significant question for those set in families to ask themselves. When we return home, will members of our domestic circle experience joy or pain? Our approach to the house where we
live may provoke stifled sighs, may even cause members of the
family to suppress a groan: "Here's that man again, with his
temper, his complaints, his whine." One uncongenial saint of an
earlier day is remembered because of a letter written to an acquaintance preceding a visit. "Be much in prayer," he admon-
ished, "for I am coming to spend the week-end with you." When
father or mother returns, will the children rejoice? Doubtless the
emotional response depends at least partly on the kind of behavior

181

in which the children have been indulging during the parent's absence. It also depends on our behavior when we are not on parade.

Will those who are engaged in the struggle for a more Christian community be glad when they see us? Will our presence signal the arrival of a public-spirited helper or a destructively critical hinderer? Pastors have confessed that when certain officials arrived for a church board meeting the silent prayer their more hopeful colleagues offered was mainly a petition for self-control and patience.

One aspect of the matter needs to be clarified at once. We have failed a test of Christian character if everyone is glad to see us. On the highest authority, we are assured that we are in a spiritually dangerous condition when all men speak well of us.[1] Now and again we encounter a person, affable, charming and expansive, who could be admitted without further examination to a master's degree in popularity. Not infrequently such pleasant souls pay too high a price for popularity. Adept in taking the color and reflecting the attitudes of any group, such agreeable persons seem incapable of asserting a different view from the majority when such a dissenting opinion is strongly indicated. Have you heard of the lady who always bowed her head in church when the devil was mentioned? Asked why she showed such respect for Satan she explained, "Well, my dear, politeness costs nothing and you'll never know where you will find yourself." A Christian ought not to be popular with all of the people all of the time, or even for much of the time. Recently I worshiped in the Washington church where one of the heads of the Federal Bureau of Investigation is an active and respected member. As I sat in the chancel during the anthem, an impious question entered my mind: "Would every member of Congress and every prominent citizen be glad if this particular representative of the forces of justice walked into his office?" This query was quickly succeeded by another, "Would the heads of national states be delighted to see the Prince of Peace enter their council rooms as

they planned foreign policy? Would *I* have no uneasiness if He
came to see me?"

In these days of widespread indifference to the claims of Christ
and His Church, a case can be made for every pastor and church
official who strives to win members and influence subscribers to
the local budget, but not at the expense of high Christian
standards. In Worcester Cathedral a stone bearing the date 1576
carries this inscription:

> Here born, here bishop,
>   buried here,
> A Bullingham by name and stock,
> A Painful Preacher of the Truth.

It is an uncommonly high tribute. True, most of us who preach
do not need to exert ourselves to qualify as painful, in the worst
sense. Nevertheless, we may assume that the good bishop was gratefully remembered by those who knew him because his loyalty to
Christ, his love of men and women in terms of what they might
become, made him spurn the utterance of innocuous platitudes
that he might declare the searching words of God. An ambassador
of Christ desires the courage to speak boldly to men's condition
even when such speaking is unsought and unwelcome. We may
be sure that not all citizens of Worcester during the ministry
of Bishop Bullingham were glad when they saw him. An animated
conscience wins few popularity prizes.

Yet the best people should have valid reason to be glad when
they see us. Men and women, boys and girls, who act as the salt
of the earth, would hail us as colleagues if we also were saints in
the making, seekers of the beloved community whose builder and
maker is God.

This conviction gripped the writer of Psalm 119, when he
made his bold declaration that "they that fear [God] will be
glad when they see me." The entire Psalm repays leisurely study,
not only because it is the longest in the Bible. His candid com-
ments on snobs and other sinners indicate that he was having a
rough time. Certainly he was not popular with many people.

When he approached a group of acquaintances, one was likely to say in a low voice, "Don't look now, but guess who's coming." Reassurance comes to his severely tested spirit when he recalls others who will be pleased to have him in their company. "They will be glad when they see me," he asserts with excusable pride. Their affectionate comradeship more than compensates for the hostility of his enemies. His words are loaded with deep satisfaction. Who are "they" that respond with such genuine friendliness? "They that fear Thee" even as this hard-beset pilgrim fears God; "they that fear Thee will be glad when they see me; because I have hoped in Thy Word."

Here is the open secret of significant popularity: to live each day as one who hopes in the living Word of God. What does this mean? It means that we have made life's greatest decision, have committed ourselves in loving trust to God our heavenly Father in Jesus Christ, and by the power of the Holy Spirit live the life of Christian love. To use the phrase of the late William Temple, Archbishop of Canterbury, it means that we have committed all that we know of ourselves to all that we know of God in Jesus Christ. To make this commitment, and to renew it by daily dedication and discipline as members of Christ's company, is to grow into the kind of person the best people like to have around. Few of his admirers would nominate the late Robert Benchley for canonization as an indubitable saint according to the traditional pattern. Yet if his fellow humorist, James Thurber, was right in his estimate, Robert Benchley possessed one essential characteristic of the Lord's merry men. "People were surprisingly improved in his company," wrote Mr. Thurber after his friend's death; "surprisingly at home on a level of easy charm of which nobody would have dreamed they were capable." Charm and grace are close relatives, and at their spiritual best derive from the divine source of grace. If you and I seriously want to be popular with the best people we need to keep close to One who more than any other enables people to be "surprisingly improved in His company."

This is no solitary exercise. Christ's presence is most truly realized within the fellowship He creates. Worshiping, witnessing,
and serving as members of His Body the Church, we find ourselves
with those whose glad approval means more than that of any
other society. Christians belong to the most meaningful and
glorious of all communities. The most congenial and inspiring
friends we can ever know are His friends. These are they who
hold the fabric of the world together, who give themselves away
to others, who maintain the moral health and spiritual vitality of
the common life. Christians are those who live as if the Kingdom
of God had already come, as indeed it has come for them through
their encounter with the living Christ. Across all boundaries of
race, class and sectarian difference this fellowship extends. Dr.
Hans Lilje, bishop of the Evangelical Lutheran Church in Ger-
many, has told of the way in which men in Nazi concentration
camps found that Who they believed mattered so much more
than what they believed about their respective churches. Ecclesiastical barriers dissolved in the fires of mutual recognition of
oneness in Christ. Roman Catholics and Protestants of various
communions discovered that they all hoped in God's Word. Faith
was to them assurance of things hoped for. As companions in
distress, each of them was "inwardly completely free, friendly,
helpful, thoughtful for others, a truly free human being, with
inward nobility in the midst of a world of meanness and cruelty."[2]
In a time of horror and deprivation each prisoner who was also
a captive of Christ could say, "They that fear the Lord are glad
when they see me, because I too hope in His Word." Under the
cross of persecution, and in every circumstance, those who reverence and love God know each other and love what they know.

Let the question apply to another dimension of life. Will the
saints in light be glad when they see us? No conception of
immortality ultimately satisfies the Christian mind which is in-
dividualistic in character. Few honestly desire life beyond this life
apart from others. There is nothing heavenly about isolation.
However little we think of the next phase of existence, when we

do we vote for an immortality in which we shall rediscover old comrades and find new ones. This is the kind of eternal life our Lord has promised. "Quiet yourself, good Master Pope," Sir Thomas More is reported to have said to a heartbroken friend as he climbed to the scaffold. "Quiet yourself and be not discomforted, for I trust that we shall in heaven see each other full merrily." Shall we? Will those who have preceded us greet us "full merrily"? Does it not depend on whether now we hope in His Word and serve Him and His children here?

In the summer of 1949 a good minister of Jesus Christ, Dr. J. R. P. Sclater, fell on sleep while visiting his beloved Scotland. For a quarter of a century he had been a singularly effective minister in the city of Toronto. Unusually gifted as a preacher, he was a churchman of vision and influence. When his death was announced, the newspapers carried many tributes to his character and work. One of the most beautiful came from a parishioner who was a patient in one of the hospitals. This man recalled the difference his friend and pastor had made in his life by his frequent visits to him. Just to see him strengthened his faith and recovered his courage, said the invalid. This is how he ended his tribute:

> Some day—it may be soon—I shall meet my friend again. He will look just the same, smiling, radiant, as the saints at rest. "Come in," he will say. "I have been looking for you. We have work for you." And I, young and strong again, will take up the humble task allotted to me.

To be that kind of person is worth everything we can give. This the divine grace enables us to do: to live and trust and toil and love through the days of our years, that when we move on, those who love God and serve Him in His near presence will be glad when they see us, because we have hoped in His Word.

PRAYER: *O God of love who knowest our deep desires and who dost answer our needs before we make them known, thanks be unto Thee for Thy gift of faith whereby we respond to Thee in trust and obedience. Grant us grace, O Lord, that we may love and serve Thee with such steadfastness and radiance that others may be glad of our presence and service. Until we all come home, hoping in Thy Word and trusting Thine unfailing love; through Jesus Christ our Lord. Amen.*

Notes*

1. BASIC CHRISTIANITY

1. Arnold J. Toynbee, *A Study of History;* abridgment by D. C. Somervell. Oxford, 1947, pp. 544, 547.
2. John 20:28 (A.V.).
3. Heb. 1:1-3.
4. John 1:14.
5. Robert Browning, "Saul," xviii.
6. "Death in the Desert."
7. Alice Meynell, *Christ in the Universe.* Reprinted with permission of Burns, Oates & Washbourne, Ltd., and Mr. Wilfred Meynell, executor.
8. Willard L. Sperry, *Jesus Then and Now.* Harper, 1949, pp. 93-94.
9. 2 Cor. 5:17.
10. Matt. 28:20.
11. T. T. Lynch, "I Have a Captain."

2. GOOD NEWS FOR "NOBODIES"

1. "I'm Nobody" from *Poems by Emily Dickinson,* edited by Martha Dickinson Bianchi and Alfred Leete Hampson. Little, Brown, 1930.
2. Rom. 5:7, 8.
3. Luke 12:6.
4. John 16:32.
5. Edward Everett Hale, "The Nameless Saints."

3. HOW CAN A MAN KNOW GOD?

1. Rev. 21:12 (A.V.).
2. Ps. 73:23, 24, 26 (Moffatt).
3. Mark 10:17-22 (A.V.).
4. John 1:14, 18.
5. 2 Cor. 4:6.
6. John 7:17.
7. 1 John 4:16.

---

* Unless otherwise indicated, Scripture quotations from the New Testament are from the *Revised Standard Version.*

8. Heb. 11:6 (A.V.).
9. John 14:21.

4. WAKE UP AND LIVE

1. Rom. 13 (Phillips).
2. Sir Walter Moberly, *The Crisis in the University*. Macmillan, 1949.
3. Christopher Fry, *The Lady's Not for Burning*. Copyright, 1949, 1950, by Oxford University Press, and reprinted with their permission.
4. Luke 9:32 (A.V.).

5. MANKIND'S UNFAILING LAMP

1. F. C. Bryan, *Concerning the Way*. S.C.M. Press, 1943, p. 53.
2. For this suggestion I am indebted to Dr. Corwin C. Roach.
3. Acts 9:2 (A.V.).
4. Roach, *Preaching Values in the Bible*. Cloister Press, 1946, p. 34.
5. John 14:6.
6. Rev. 21:2.
7. Isa. 35:10 (A.V.).

6. CHRISTMAS UNLIMITED

1. Cf. John 1:14.
2. John 4:14; 7:37, 39 (A.V.).
3. John 14:18.
4. John 17:26.

7. WHERE DID CHRISTMAS GO?

1. George Edward Hoffman, "December 26." Reprinted with permission of the poet.
2. John Oxenham, "How—When—Where." Reprinted with permission of Erica Oxenham.
3. 1 Cor. 10:31 (A.V.).
4. Matt. 2:13 (A.V.).
5. Luke 2:40 (A.V.).
6. Eleanor Slater, "December Twenty-fourth," from *Why Hold the Hound?* Copyright, 1941, by Exposition Press, Inc., and reprinted with their permission.
7. Phil. 2:6, 7 (A.V.).
8. Giles Fletcher, Jr., "Christ's Victorie and Triumph in Heaven and Earth."
9. In John Masefield, *The Trial of Jesus*. Macmillan, 1925.

8. A Condition Men Forget

1. Earl Stanley B. Baldwin, *Sir Robert Falconer Lectures*. University of Toronto Press, 1939.
2. Matt. 5:23 (A.V.).
3. Walter Eccles, "Not Understood."

9. Religion without Tears

1. Aldous Huxley, *Brave New World*. Harper, 1946, pp. 285-88.
2. Hubert L. Simpson, *The Intention of His Soul*. Hodder & Stoughton, 1924, p. 127.
3. John 6:60 (A.V.).
4. Willard L. Sperry, *Those of the Way*. Harper, 1945, p. 85.
5. Matt. 7:13, 14.
6. William Clow, *The Cross in Christian Experience*. Harper, 1928, p. 236.
7. 2 Sam. 24:24.

10. Heartbreak Hill

1. Edith Lovejoy Pierce, "Heartbreak Ridge," in *The Christian Century*, March 26, 1952. Reprinted with permission of the poet.
2. Eph. 6:12.
3. Heb. 12:3.
4. Leila Avery Rotherburger, "Three Crosses."
5. Rom. 14:17.
6. Rom. 5:6-8.
7. Acts 5:30, 31.
8. 2 Cor. 5:17, 18.
9. 2 Cor. 5:14, 15.
10. Col. 2:13-15.
11. 1 Cor. 15:25.
12. Rev. 11:15.

11. The Secret Society

1. Matt. 13:11 (Goodspeed).
2. Christina Georgina Rossetti, "None Other Lamb."

12. I Saw Two Calvaries

1. John Knox, *The Man Christ Jesus*. Harper, 1941, p. 67.
2. G. A. Studdert-Kennedy, *The Word and the Work*. Longmans, 1925, pp. 57, 58.

3. *Ibid.,* p. 58.

4. Luke 22:53.

5. "Heil, Heilige Nacht" from *Good Intentions.* Copyright, 1942, by Ogden Nash and reprinted with permission of Little, Brown & Company.

6. Col. 2:15.

13. "ONLY THE TRUTH REMAINS"

1. From "Good Friday," in *Poems* by John Masefield. Copyright, 1935, and reprinted with permission of the Macmillan Company.

2. "Abt Vogler," xii.

3. In *Testament of Love.* Hodder & Stoughton, 1934.

4. Robert Browning, "Rest Remaineth."

14. PRESENT—TENSE; FUTURE—PERFECT

1. Mary E. McCullough, "Thought for Easter." Reprinted with permission of the late poet's mother, Mrs. G. A. McCullough.

2. Reprinted with permission of the poet.

3. John R. Slater, "An Easter Reveille." Reprinted with permission of the poet.

15. WHY DID HE RETURN?

1. Acts 1:3 (Goodspeed).

2. Thomas Tiplady, "When the Daylight Wanes" from *Hymns for the Times.* Copyright, 1918, by Epworth Press. Reprinted with permission of Thomas Tiplady.

3. "No Distant Lord," from *Thoughts for Everyday Living* by Maltbie D. Babcock. Copyright, 1901, by Charles Scribner's Sons, 1929, by Katherine T. Babcock. Used by permission of the publishers.

4. McEwan Lawson in *The Christian World*, March 31, 1949.

16. "CAN THESE BONES LIVE?"

1. Acts 2:38.

2. Harriet Auber, "The Holy Spirit."

3. Francis Thompson, "Lilium Regis."

17. WHY THE CHURCH?

1. Eph. 5:25.

2. T. S. Eliot, *The Rock,* vii. Copyright, 1934, by Harcourt, Brace and Company, Inc., and reprinted with permission of Harcourt, Brace and Company and Faber and Faber, Ltd.

3. Peter Gething, "Prayer."

18. PUTTING THINGS RIGHT

1. Amos 5:15.
2. Matt. 23:27.
3. Rudyard Kipling, "The Prodigal Son," from *Kim*. Copyright, 1900, 1901, by Rudyard Kipling. Reprinted with permission of Mrs. George Bambridge, Doubleday & Company, Inc., The Macmillan Company of Canada, and A. P. Watt & Son.
4. Mark 3:5.
5. A. P. Herbert, *Independent Member*. Doubleday, 1951, p. 91.
6. Matt. 5:22 (Moffatt).
7. E. Stanley Jones, *The Way*. Abingdon-Cokesbury, 1946, p. 105.
8. James A. Fraser, "Apprehension." Reprinted with permission of *The Presbyterian Tribune*.

19. QUESTIONS BEFORE THE HOUSE

1. Dwight D. Eisenhower, *Crusade in Europe*. Heinemann, 1951, p. 389.

20. THE NECESSITY OF COMRADESHIP

1. George Matheson, "Gather Us In."

21. THE "THIN THREAD OF THANKS"

1. Eph. 5:20 (Goodspeed).
2. *In the Secret Place of the Most High*. Scribner's, 1948.

22. HOW TO BE POPULAR WITH THE BEST PEOPLE

1. Luke 6:26 (A.V.).
2. Hans Lilje, *The Valley of the Shadow*. S.C.M. Press, 1950, p. 71.

Index